Another Red Letter Day

A study of John 14, 15 and 16

By

Jeffrey Kobman

Another Red Letter Day

Copyright © 2022

Jeffrey D. Kobman

All Rights Reserved

Dedication

I dedicate this book to my pastors and friends, Richard and Christine Dunk. I did this because my relationship with them is priceless. They taught me the Word of God, making it a book of more than words about God and revealing to me that it is a spiritual union between God and the believer. They took the time to spoon-feed the milk of the Word and brought me to the solid food of the Word. As skillful pastors full of the Holy Spirit of God, they knew when to feed milk and when it was time for solid food. They encouraged, corrected and prayed for me. They stood with me through thick and thin and helped develop me into the man of God I am today.

Saying "thanks" is insufficient so I will add this. I want to say thank you for listening to God and shepherding me. Thank you for teaching me always to follow God regardless of the cost. Thank you for demonstrating Jesus to me with and in your life – your words and deeds. Thank you for being faithful friends.

Jeffrey Kobman

Spotsylvania, Virginia

August 2022

Bible Copyrights

The following versions of the Bible were used in this book. The author wishes to thank the Bible translators for their diligence in assembling these versions of the Holy Bible to bring glory to God.

KJV - King James Version

Scripture quotations marked "KJV" are taken from the Holy Bible, King James Version, Cambridge, 1769.

NLT - New Living Translation

Scripture quotations marked "NLT" are taken from the Holy Bible, New Living Translation, copyright 1996. Used by permission of Tyndale House Publishers, Inc., Wheaton, Illinois 60189. All rights reserved.

NIV - New International Version

Scripture quotations marked "NIV" are taken from HOLY BIBLE, NEW INTERNATIONAL VERSION. Copyright 1973, 1978, 1984 by International Bible Society. Used by permission of Zondervan Publishing House.

MSG – The Message
Scripture taken from *THE MESSAGE*. Copyright © 1993, 1994, 1995, 1996, 2000, 2001, 2002. Used by permission of NavPress Publishing Group.

ESV - The Holy Bible: English Standard Version

Scripture quotations marked "ESV" are taken from The Holy Bible: English Standard Version, copyright 2001, Wheaton: Good News Publishers. Used by permission. All rights reserved.

AMP - The Amplified Bible

Scripture quotations marked "The Amplified Bible" or "The Amplified New Testament" are taken from The Amplified Bible, Old Testament copyright 1965, 1987 by the Zondervan Corporation and The Amplified New Testament copyright 1958, 1987 by The Lockman Foundation. Used by permission. All rights reserved.

Foreword

My husband, Fred and I have had the privilege of knowing Jeffrey for several years. We have known him to be an honest and sincere man of God, faithful in his personal life, and in his local church. His teachings are thorough, well studied, and easily understood. He uses illustrations from his own personal relationship with God to make his message relatable to even the youngest of believers. He has taught in several African Bible schools affiliated with us, and is a passionate teacher and scholar, well loved by our students for his understanding of God's Word.

While reading "Another Red Letter Day," a study of John 14, 15, and 16, I was impressed by one specific thread that is woven throughout the book. That is TRUTH. Jeff shows the truth of who our loving God is, that there is only one way to Him, and how to live for Him. In stories from his own life and relationships, he explains the truth of our destiny, covenant relationship, and the power of Christ in us through the working of the Holy Spirit. He summed it all up well when he said, "Abiding in His love involves having an ongoing relationship with Him."

This book is for all of those interested in understanding the last few hours of Jesus's life just before he went to the cross. It is for anyone hungry to know the truth of God's amazing love, shown through the words of Jesus as He poured out His heart to those closest to Him. Open your heart and your Bible as you read "Another Red Letter Day" and watch the truth change your life.

Debby Davis

Author of: Keepers Of Salt,

Suddenly, Creatures of the

Forest, and more.

Table of Contents

John 14

Chapter		Page
One	The Four Important Truths	15
Two	A Relationship With God	25
Three	Father, Son And Holy Spirit	37
Four	The Way, The Truth And The Life	55
Five	The Comforter	65
Six	A Man Of God	85
Seven	Obey His Commands	107
Eight	I Am Going Away	121
Nine	The Peace Of God	137
Ten	God Puts Dreams In Your Heart	153

John 15

Chapter		Page
One	The Real Thing	167
Two	God Loves Trees	175
Three	We Are Growing Fruit	185
Four	Enabled by God	195
Five	Abide In My Love	203
Six	Greater Love	211
Seven	Appointed To Bear Fruit	219
Eight	They Hated Me	231
Nine	Written In Their Love	241

| Ten | The Holy Spirit Will Come | 247 |

John 16

Chapter		**Page**
One	Where Will We Go?	259
Two	Hear Me Now	267
Three	It's Time For Me To Go	275
Four	Sin, Righteousness And Judgement	285
Five	See Me And Not See Me	295
Six	No One Can Rob You Of That Joy	305
Seven	Now It's All Clear	313
Eight	You Will Be Scattered	321

| | **Do You Know Jesus?** | 329 |

Another Red Letter Day
Introduction

Calendars always feature red-letter days. The numbers are printed in red and signify holidays and days that are celebrated. These days are set apart from the other days because red-letter days are special!

Every society is different. They celebrate different holidays because of their importance. Red-letter days in America include the 4th of July, Thanksgiving, Christmas and Easter. There are other holidays, but these are the most popular red-letter days.

As a kid, I always looked forward to these red-letter days because my family would gather – grandparents, my aunt and uncle and cousins. Of course, there was an amazing spread of food (including pies and "bumpy cake"), games, lots of pictures and a full day of fun!

Many Bible versions feature "the Words of Christ in red." This is embossed on the binding and printed on the title page. Every time Jesus spoke, the words are printed with red ink. So, John 3:16 (and the rest of Jesus' dialogue in the book of John) are red. This shows that these words are unique and separate from the writer's descriptions and commentary.

Every day that I read my Bible and see the words of Christ in red is special. It's a day to celebrate and be with Jesus.

Jesus took special time with His disciples in the scenes described in this book. He was sharing His life and the essential things that they would experience from that night forward. My dad would say that Jesus was giving them their "marching orders."

Jesus was talking to His followers and we talk to Him. People must understand that being allowed to talk to God is only because Jesus purchased us from sin. We fellowship with Jesus when we pray (talk) to God, spend time with other believers and read the Word of God.

These truths in John 14, 15 and 16 are spoken and written to disciples to help them know that He was leaving to go to the Father and He would send the Holy Spirit. Please allow the Holy Spirit to pour these truths into your life so they become a part of you.

I hope that you enjoy reading this book as much as I enjoyed writing it. Remember, every day is *Another Red Letter Day* with Jesus.

John 14 Preface

One of the first scriptures that many young Christians learn is John 14:6.

> Jesus told him, "I am the way, the truth, and the life. No one can come to the Father except through me. (John 14:6 NLT)

Even though I attended church for years, I was amazed to know that Jesus Himself was the only Way to God, the only Truth to speak and live and the only Life that was worthy to be lived. I learned that I could not live for God unless I went to God through Jesus Christ.

Jesus talks to us about the Father and the Holy Spirit. God was not some unclear concept that could not be understood; He is a spiritual person who is alive and real. The Holy Spirit would be the personal God who would connect every believer with God.

These words were some of the last things that Jesus would speak to His disciples before He was arrested, tried, tortured and killed by crucifixion. These same essential words are spoken to each individual believer. These words are meant to inform the believer and help Him grow and know that being a believer is not a religion. It is a relationship with God.

Read John 14 and grow in your relationship with God.

John 14
Chapter 1
The 4 Important Truths

What are the 4 Important Truths?

1. God is Real.
2. The Bible is True.
3. God wants a relationship with you.
4. God speaks with you.

Why are these 4 Truths important? They are *essential*, *established*, and *accepted,* and they are the truths of the Bible. Answering this question is complex yet simple. They are complex because God's ways are much higher than man's. He is incomprehensible to human reasoning. They are simple because He reaches out and reveals Himself to us personally and meets us at the point of our need. And He meets us exactly where we are.

These Truths are the core belief of being a Christian. It is not open for debate whether God exists or the Bible is true. Everyone has a right to their personal opinion, and I respect that. But I am not convinced of the correctness of someone's opinion concerning these Truths. The Scriptures are true, and God is real.

Jesus told us what we should receive from God's Word.

> Sanctify them by Your Truth. Your word is Truth. (John 17:17 NKJV)

Believers receive sanctification from God Almighty.

Sanctify means to separate yourself from profane and unholy things that are disrespectful towards God. Someone who is sanctified has been dedicated to God. They are set apart from the evil that is in the world and from the godless ways of people. Instead, the sanctified person is dedicated by God to follow the purposes He designed for them. The truths of the Bible apply to the entire Body of Christ and are written in the Bible.

My personal experience with God has taught me that I can totally trust the Bible and read it as God's message to me. We also listen for the "still small voice" (1 Kings 19:11-13 NKJV) of the Holy Spirit as He leads us and guides us. Believers need to listen to God more and <u>not</u> listen to the profane, unholy and anti-God things the world tells us.

God's "still small voice" will <u>always</u> tell you things that agree with the Bible. For instance,

God will never tell you to worship a false God or to forsake Jesus Christ. Rather, we fear God (have a deep loving respect for Him) in every aspect of our life.

> The fear of the LORD *is* clean, enduring forever; The judgments of the LORD *are* true *and* righteous altogether. (Psalm 19:9 NKJV)

Fearing God is not being scared of Him. We love Him so much that we desire to do what He says.

The Bible is true and we can be confident in God that we will always hear truthful words from Him. God will never send you away from Him, but always lead you to Him. We can approach Him because of the redemption we have in Jesus Christ. We are of His Truth - a part of His "crowd" who know Him.

> Everyone who is of the Truth hears My voice. (John 18:37b NKJV)

> All who love the Truth recognize that what I say is true. (John 18:37b NLT)

Simply stated, Jesus wants us to believe Him. He clearly tells us that He is the Son of God and is ready to help those who believe.

> Believe Me that I *am* in the Father and the Father in Me, or else believe Me for

the sake of the works themselves. (John 14:11 NKJV)

Jesus said it and His followers believe it.

Unbelievers can choose to receive Jesus as their Savior. This is the entry point for believing and coming to faith in God. This scripture above tells us that we can believe Him because of His words and His miracles. These words and miracles came from God. It is simply a matter of surrendering to Him and receiving Him as Savior and Lord.

Some people see Jesus as only being divine (God) and others as only a man (human). Jesus was entirely God and entirely man – 100% God and 100% man. Believers trust that God sent Jesus personally for each of us to redeem us, change us, heal us and baptize us in His Holy Spirit. Believers know that Jesus is in the Father and the Father is in Him.

Belief or unbelief tells us exactly where we are with Christ. We are either "in Him" (belief) or not. Jesus will welcome believers at the second coming or He will tell people at the judgment, "I never knew you" (unbelief). We are either believers or unbelievers.

These 4 Important Truths serve as guideposts or road signs in the life of a Christian. These Truths will help every believer to know if where they are going in life is correct or if they need to change course. Guideposts and road signs help us know whether we should <u>stop</u> where we are or just <u>keep going</u>.

The 4 Important Truths tell us that the Bible is accurate and true. This is clearly seen when Jesus told us that He is the Truth. (John 14:6) The believer hears the Truth directly from God, the same Truth that is spoken to every follower of Jesus.

I want God's guidance. I want to know the leading of the Holy Spirit in every part of my life, both big things and the small things. God loves His children and cares about every aspect of their lives.

A believer might ask, "how can I know God's will?" The *4 Important Truths* provide direction for our lives as we live for God. This direction offers the information that is His will for us.

These Truths in our lives will help the believer to know what they believe. The Truths can serve as a basic guideline to follow as we serve God and help people. For example, if someone asked me what they should do in a situation, I would mention what the Bible says. If they say, "I don't believe in God" I would tell them why I believe in God and concentrate on what the Scriptures say. You can't make someone believe, but <u>you</u> can hold on to what you believe. If you know that God is real and the Bible is true, then keep that belief in your life by living it every day.

Because the Bible is true and God speaks to us, we can hold fast to the Truth of the Word of God. *Read the Bible and know the Truth.* It sounds like a religious slogan, but it's an eternal principle - Truth from God is available to everyone and applies to believers and unbelievers alike.

> Thy word is a lamp unto my feet, and a light unto my path. I have sworn, and I will perform it, that I will keep thy righteous judgments. (Psalm 119:105-106 KJV)
>
> Your word is a lamp to guide my feet and a light for my path. I've promised it once, and I'll promise it again: I will obey your righteous regulations. (Psalm 119:105-106 NLT)
>
> By your words I can see where I'm going; they throw a beam of light on my dark path. I've committed myself and I'll never turn back from living by your righteous order. (Psalm 119:105-106 MSG)

The 4 Important Truths will also bring specific guidance. "Should I move to New York or stay here?" As we build a relationship with God, we will hear His direction. In this, we must always respect God's reasons and timing. He says "GO" we go and He says "STOP" we stop.

Sometimes life is easy – there are no real hassles or challenges. But sometimes life is a real challenge – it's just one BIG problem after another. It's like trying to climb up the face of Niagara Falls with the torrent of water crashing down on you – this is an impossible task. But because of His Word guiding us (like a light on our path!), we become keenly aware of His presence, His ability to work things out and that all is well because of Him.

God wants a relationship with all people, especially with you! IF you don't know Jesus, receive Him today.

IF you need to be baptized in the Holy Spirit, don't wait. Receive Him today. God brings us to Him through Jesus Christ. John 3:16-17 tells us about His love and that He did not come to condemn us to a death sentence. Rather, Jesus came to give us eternal life with Him. He seeks us as He reaches out to us. In this beautiful relationship we have with Him, God richly blesses us.

Chapter Questions for Discussion or Study

1. Choose one of the 4 Important Truths and describe why it is important to you.

2. How is the word *sanctify* meaningful to you?

3. We saw that "the Bible is True." When have you experienced this Truth?

4. Our relationship with God is personal. We must share the Gospel with others. How have you shared your personal beliefs and helped others to believe?

5. Why does God speak to His people?

6. In what ways does God speak to believers?

7. How is knowing the Truth important in hearing from God?

8. Explain how a believer can use the 4 Important Truths as a guidepost to help direct your life.

9. A lamp or flashlight guides a person down a dark path. How does God's Word guide you?

10. Specific guidance from God is essential to the believer. Can you describe a time when God guided you?

John 14
Chapter 2
A Relationship With God

In my second book, *A Strong Relationship With God*, we examined the different factors that determine a strong, robust and living relationship with God. We looked at Hebrews 11 and other scriptures to examine the lives of people who accepted God's invitation to enter into a relationship. This chapter mentions many people whose life stories are well known.

- Abel offered a better sacrifice that God accepted. Cain was angry and killed Abel.
- Enoch pleased God and was taken from the earth. Enoch never saw death.
- Noah understood and believed God. He wanted Noah to build an ark. Though a near-impossible task, Noah followed and completed God's call. Noah rescued his family and many animals from the judgment of the flood.

- Abraham was faithful and obeyed God. He followed God's leading and was a friend of God.
- Many other people were specifically mentioned as people who obeyed and followed God faithfully.
- Some of these people were listed in Hebrews 11 because they trusted God and lost their life.

All of these people in Hebrews 11 had something in common – they lived their faith in God. This faith in God inspired them to follow God regardless of the extreme personal cost to themselves and their families. Faith will cause you to follow God regardless of the cost.

The Bible is full of people who dared to believe that God exists and that He rewards people for their faith in Him.

> And it is impossible to please God without faith. Anyone who wants to come to him must believe that God exists and that he rewards those who sincerely seek him. (Hebrews 11:6 NLT)

This relationship with God sets a man or woman apart from those who do not believe. It's as if the righteous people. They treat righteous people who follow Christ as if they are from another planet. The righteous choose to believe in an unseen God who speaks to them. This was particularly true of Abraham.

> What then shall we say that Abraham, our forefather according to the flesh, discovered in this matter? If, in fact, Abraham was justified by works, he had something to boast about - but not before God. What does Scripture say? "Abraham believed God, and it was credited to him as righteousness." (Romans 4:1-3 ESV)

> That is why it depends on faith, in order that the promise may rest on grace and be guaranteed to all his offspring - not only to the adherent of the law but also to the one who shares the faith of Abraham, who is the father of us all, (Romans 4:16 ESV)

Abraham stands out from other people in the Bible because of his faith. He and his family left their home and followed God. Even though God had not revealed his destination, Abraham followed God's direction by faith. This took courage and this type of courage that only comes through faith in God.

Abraham's righteousness came from God. His righteousness was a gift from God, not because he earned it. It was all because he dared to believe God.

When a believer decides to receive and follow Christ as Savior and Lord, they are made righteous.

> God made him who had no sin to be sin for us, so that in him we might become the righteousness of God. (2 Corinthians 5:21 NIV)

> For God made Christ, who never sinned, to be the offering for our sin, so that we could be made right with God through Christ. (2 Corinthians 5:21 NLT)

Righteousness is a condition where we are restored to a place before God just as if we had never sinned. Our sins are forgiven and we are made righteous when we are washed in the blood of Jesus Christ.

One huge question remains – why does God want a relationship with us? Why would a holy God come to earth and sacrifice Jesus for <u>our</u> sins? Why would He do all of this to make us righteous, right with God?

> But God showed his great love for us by sending Christ to die for us while we were still sinners. (Romans 5:8 NLT)

> But God put his love on the line for us by offering his Son in sacrificial death while we were of no use whatever to him. (Romans 5:8 MSG)

It was because of God's great love for each of us that He sent Jesus Christ to the cross to die for all people for all time. This includes the past, present and future. All it involves to receive eternal life from God is to receive Jesus Christ as Savior and Lord.

When Adam and Eve disobeyed God and sinned (Genesis 3), their eyes were opened. Their disobedience and sin brought separation between them and God. This sin and separation came upon us because we are members of the human race. But God already had a plan to restore the relationship!

When we are a part of a relationship, we choose to treat the person well and develop loyalty towards them. We treat others in the same way as we want to be treated. This is known as the Golden Rule (Matthew 7:12). As one person told me, "I will make the Golden Rule my daily rule." This is a matter of respect for others and how we treat our friends.

Friends have mutual trust and respect for each other. This is a critical factor in a relationship. As we treat others well and practice the Golden Rule, we both benefit because we develop a connection with the other person.

Abraham was called a friend of God.

> And the scripture was fulfilled that says, "Abraham believed God, and it was credited to him as righteousness," and he was called God's friend. (James 2:23 NIV)

In the case of Abraham and God, they had a close relationship that developed into a lasting friendship.

> The LORD had said to Abram, "Go from your country, your people and your father's household to the land I will show you. (Genesis 12:1 NIV)

> So, Abram went, as the LORD had told him; and Lot went with him. Abram was seventy-five years old when he set out from Harran. (Genesis 12:4 NIV)

Abraham left his home for an unknown destination. This took a firm trust in God and genuine courage to believe God. If I am told to move from my home, I want to know where I am going. But sometimes God gives people direction and doesn't tell them *why* – He is God Almighty and doesn't need to explain Himself. This is where faith in God to trust Him comes in. In the case of Abraham, God sent him out without much information. God did not give him a roadmap or a list of places he would go. I tend to think that God revealed His direction little by little as He moved Abraham along. We can say that Abraham "walked by faith" - he trusted God to care for and protect him without a sense of clear direction or long-term travel goals. He was a friend of God.

Years later, these two friends entered into a covenant.

> When Abram was ninety-nine years old, the LORD appeared to him and said, "I am God Almighty; walk before me faithfully and be blameless. Then I will make my covenant between me and you and will greatly increase your numbers." (Genesis 17:1-2 NIV)

> This is my covenant with you: I will make you the father of a multitude of nations! What's more, I am changing your name. It will no longer be Abram. Instead, you will be called Abraham, for you will be the father of many nations. (Genesis 17:4-5 NLT)

Within the covenant that they made, God pledged to make Abraham who had no children, the father of many nations. God knew that Abraham trusted Him and had clearly proved it down through the years. When it came time, God called Abraham to offer his son Isaac.

> God said to him, "Abraham!" "Here I am," he replied. Then God said, "Take your son, your only son, whom you love - Isaac and go to the region of Moriah. Sacrifice him there as a burnt offering on a mountain I will show you." (Genesis 22:1-2 NIV)

Abraham obeyed God in spite of the high personal cost of sacrificing Isaac. God stopped Abraham and sent a ram for the sacrifice.

> "Do not lay a hand on the boy," he said. "Do not do anything to him. Now I know that you fear God, because you have not withheld from me your son, your only son." Abraham looked up and there in a thicket he saw a ram caught by its horns. He went over and took the ram and sacrificed it as a burnt offering instead of his son. (Genesis 22:12-13 NIV)

God called Abraham to this extremely difficult task and God provided the sacrifice. All of this was due to their friendship and the covenant that they had made. Both of them brought something for the sacrifice. Abraham obeyed God by bringing Isaac and God provided a ram.

At an even greater cost and a triumphant final outcome, God sent His son Jesus to die for the sins of everyone. The major difference was that a substitute sacrifice didn't appear to rescue Jesus from crucifixion. God the Father followed through and sacrificed Jesus. Jesus obeyed His heavenly Father and willingly went to the cross.

> What we do see is Jesus, who for a little while was given a position "a little lower than the angels"; and because he suffered death for us, he is now "crowned with glory and honor." Yes, by God's grace, Jesus tasted death for everyone. (Hebrews 2:9 NLT)

Jesus the sinless Son of God experienced death for everyone, knowing that His sacrifice would be a "game-changer." Jesus brought change to man's relationship with God. His death and resurrection bought freedom for man from sin, redemption and eternal life from God. No longer was man condemned – but now man was made righteous before God.

> And it was only right that he should make Jesus, through his suffering, a perfect leader, fit to bring them into their salvation. (Hebrews 2:10b NLT)

Why did God desire a relationship with Abraham as He also did with Enoch? Enoch walked "faithfully" and "in close fellowship" with God. (Genesis 5:24 NIV and NLT) We see this same type of relationship between God and Noah.

> Noah was a righteous man, blameless among the people of his time, and he walked faithfully with God. (Genesis 6:9 NIV)

> This is the account of Noah and his family. Noah was a righteous man, the only blameless person living on earth at the time, and he walked in close fellowship with God. (Genesis 6:9 NLT)

The relationships between God and Abraham, Enoch and Noah were all based on faith and friendship. This is the same relationship that every believer has with God. If you are a Christian, you have a relationship with God. Are you a friend of God? Has your relationship with God grown beyond the beginning when you first met God in salvation? Have you developed a friendship where talking and listening to God is a regular part of your life?

Our friendship with God brings us into a peaceful, restful relationship.

> Then Jesus said, "Come to me, all of you who are weary and carry heavy burdens, and I will give you rest. Take my yoke upon you. Let me teach you, because I am humble and gentle at

heart, and you will find rest for your souls. (Matthew 11:28-29 NLT)

We leave the hustle-bustle of our everyday lives and enter a new life. In this new life we are yoked together with Him.

I encourage you today to seek God and grow your relationship with Him. Your life will still have its' share of challenges, but you and God will walk together through this life and for eternity.

Chapter Questions for Discussion or Study

1. Choose one of the people from Hebrews 11 and tell did they live out their faith.

2. How does the person you chose help you live out your faith in God?

3. Our relationship with God sets us apart from other people. Explain how this is true in your life?

4. Why does God lead believers to follow Him without a clear outcome or destination? How have you had to trust God in this way?

5. Jesus called the disciples friends (John 15:15). Is this a greater relationship than being a *follower* of Jesus? Why?

6. What is a *covenant*? How has this affected your life?

7. How does God's covenant with Abraham relate to Jesus going to be sacrificed on the cross?

8. Why are the crucifixion and resurrection a "game-changer" for all people?

9. Why did God establish a relationship with Abraham? Why does He desire a relationship with you?

10. How is our friendship with God a peaceful, restful relationship?

John 14 Chapter 3 God The Father, God The Son And God The Holy Spirit

The 14th chapter of John is interesting because Jesus mentions the Father, the Holy Spirit and Himself, the Son of God, all in one chapter. The concept of the *Trinity* makes Christianity different – one God in three persons. The Father in heaven, the Son of God who came to earth and the Holy Spirit who abides with us and lives in us. Jesus taught this to His disciples during His ministry. This revelation was one of the new things taught and written in the Gospels.

The words of Jesus in the four Gospels were spoken before His death and resurrection. It was still the time under the Old Covenant just prior to the New Covenant that He brought. During this time before the resurrection, the disciples were learning about the Heavenly Father, the Holy Spirit and that Jesus was much more than a teacher and prophet that God sent. We now know that Jesus Christ was the anointed Son of God sent on a mission to earth. Jesus fully accomplished His mission – to seek and save the lost people of this earth. (Luke 19:10)

Jesus brought the New Covenant from God the Father. He entered into this Covenant with His followers, the disciples. Jesus shared bread and wine with them to confirm this covenant.

> He took some bread and gave thanks to God for it. Then he broke it into pieces and gave it to the disciples, saying, "This is my body, which is given for you. Do this to remember me." After supper he took another cup of wine and said, "This cup is the new covenant between God and his people-an agreement confirmed with my blood, which is poured out as a sacrifice for you. (Luke 22:19-20 NLT)

The New Covenant was made with the disciples at the Passover dinner. Believers today are His disciples. This New Covenant is made with every believer, the Body of Christ, on earth and in heaven.

Jesus brought the New Covenant for Israel and Judah, but they rejected it when they rejected Jesus as Messiah and Lord.

> "The day is coming," says the LORD, "when I will make a new covenant with the people of Israel and Judah. This covenant will not be like the one I made with their ancestors when I took them by the hand and brought them out of the land of Egypt. They broke that covenant, though I loved them as a husband loves his wife," says the LORD. "But this is the new covenant I will make with the people of Israel after those days," says the LORD. "I will put my instructions deep within them, and I will write them on their hearts. I will be their God, and they will be my people. (Jeremiah 31:31-33 NLT)
>
> But in fact, the ministry Jesus has received is as superior to theirs as the covenant of which he is mediator is superior to the old one, since the new covenant is established on better promises. For if there had been nothing wrong with that first covenant, no place would have been sought for another. (Hebrews 8:6-7 NIV)

The New Covenant was a better covenant based on the better promises of Christ.

> For God so loved the world that He gave His only begotten Son, that whoever believes in Him should not perish but have everlasting life. For God did not send His Son into the world to condemn the world, but that the world through Him might be saved. (John 3:16-17 NKJV)

God made this better promise with man because He personally loved us. God's love was constant despite the sin committed by Adam and Eve that came to the entire human race. He sacrificed Jesus on the cross and then raised Him from the dead so that mankind was no longer condemned by the tragedy of sin. The gift of forgiveness of sins and eternal life was made under the New Covenant.

Christ was the "game-changer" for everyone on earth. No longer would sin control people. Now the Father, Son and Holy Spirit would lead us. Because of this, people were made free and had a relationship with God.

Look at a few of these examples of a relationship with God.

- <u>Believers are now *in Christ*</u> - Therefore, if anyone is in Christ, the new creation has come: The old has gone, the new is here! (2 Corinthians 5:17 NIV)

- <u>Believers are connected to the life source of the True Vine</u> - I am the vine; you are the branches. If you remain in me and I in you, you will bear much fruit; apart from me you can do nothing. If you remain in me and my words remain in you, ask whatever you wish, and it will be done for you. (John 15:5,7 NIV)
- <u>Believers will carry the Good News to the people of the world</u> - And He said to them, "Go into all the world and preach the gospel to all creation. (Mark 16:15 AMP)
- <u>Believers will be saved</u> - He who has believed [in Me] and has been baptized will be saved [from the penalty of God's wrath and judgment], but he who has not believed will be condemned. (Mark 16:16 AMP)
- <u>Believers will bring the works of Christ to the people of all nations</u>. These signs will accompany those who have believed: in My name they will cast out demons, they will speak in new tongues; they will pick up serpents, and if they drink anything deadly, it will not hurt them; they will lay hands on the sick, and they will get well. (Mark 16:17-18 AMP)
- <u>Believers will live eternally with God</u> - After this I saw a vast crowd, too great to count, from every nation and tribe and

> people and language, standing in front of the throne and before the Lamb. They were clothed in white robes and held palm branches in their hands. And they were shouting with a great roar, "Salvation comes from our God who sits on the throne and from the Lamb!" (Revelation 7:9-10 NLT)

This is the wonderful thing that God did for man. It solved the HUGE problem of sin, and it was all because of God's love.

> Jesus looked at them and said, "With man this is impossible, but with God all things are possible. (Matthew 19:26 NIV)

God changed the impossible to possible for everyone everywhere through Jesus Christ. (John 14:6, 2 Corinthians 5:17)

Jesus taught us about His relationship with the Father.

> Don't cling to me, Jesus said, for I haven't yet ascended to the Father. But go find my brothers and tell them, I am ascending to my Father and your Father, to my God and your God. (John 20:17 NLT)

The heavenly Father is also <u>our</u> Father and our God.

> And I give them eternal life, and they shall never perish; neither shall anyone snatch them out of My hand. My Father, who has given *them* to Me, is greater than all; and no one is able to snatch *them* out of My Father's hand. I and *My* Father are one. (John 10:28-30 NKJV)

We are held in the hands of Jesus. Our security is guaranteed and promised by Jesus in the Word of God.

When Thomas the disciple asked Jesus about how they would know the way so they could follow Him to where He was going. Jesus told them that He was the <u>only</u> means of getting to the Father. (John 14:5-6) The disciples were not fully aware of "who" Jesus was. When asked, Peter said that Jesus was the Messiah (Christ).

> Then he asked them, "But who do you say I am? Simon Peter answered, "You are the Messiah, the Son of the living God." (Matthew 16:15-16 NLT)

In this verse, Messiah and Christ both mean *the anointed one.* The anointed is the one God appoints for a special purpose. In this case, it refers to Jesus *Christ* (Jesus the *anointed* one). He was empowered to bring God's presence and power to the people of earth.

Jesus told them (John 14:7) that they needed to know who He was. Then they would know the Father.

> If you had known Me, you would have known my Father also; and from now on you know Him and have seen Him. (John 14:7b NKJV)

We know the Father because we know Jesus. Our relationship with Jesus brings us into a relationship with the Father.

The disciples still had more questions. Phillip asked Jesus to show them the Father "and we will be satisfied." (John 14:8 NLT) It seems like the disciples had not listened to anything Jesus had told them. Jesus told them – "If you really knew me, you would know my Father as well."

This is the case when people look at a believer and think they are someone special because they have so much knowledge about God. A believer has a relationship with God through Jesus Christ; when we spend time with Him, we learn about Him. Jesus stated it accurately to the disciples and to all believers. "No one gets to the Father apart from me." (John 14:6b MSG) We receive Jesus, develop a relationship with God, and learn from God. We learn about Him, about His character and we learn about His love. He teaches and we learn.

Jesus told the disciples to take Him at His Word. This is the same way Jesus tells every believer to trust what is written in the Bible. It is more than simply accepting or giving mental assent to the idea that Jesus did a lot of significant miracles. It involves having and living with an active, all-day and everyday confidence in God. This confidence brings a deep understanding of His goodness and that He will do the same for every believer.

> who Himself bore our sins in His own body on the tree, that we, having died to sins, might live for righteousness - by whose stripes you were healed. (1 Peter 2:24 NKJV)

> He used his servant body to carry our sins to the Cross so we could be rid of sin, free to live the right way. His wounds became your healing. (1 Peter 2:24 MSG)

The Bible is the Word of God and throughout the Gospels, it clearly tells us the truth about Jesus.

- He took every one of our sins upon Himself.
- Because of this, we are freed from sin and saved.

- We are now made righteous by Jesus' death and resurrection.
- Through His wounding and terrible suffering, we are healed.
- Jesus brings us to the Father.

These statements are true. People need to change or adjust their beliefs and thinking to agree with what God says. Church doctrine and theological convictions are often at odds with the Scriptures. It is the responsibility of every disciple to believe what Jesus tells us. Jesus told the disciples that evening and is telling us today to take Him at His Word and believe Him because of His miraculous works.

As *believers*, we choose to *believe* Jesus. *Believe* and *believeth* in John 14:11-12 is a form of the Greek word *pistis* which means to have faith in, to think to be true, to be persuaded of, to validate and place confidence in. God is asking all His disciples to have faith in His ability and His love, to be persuaded that the Father sent him and that He is 100% effective in His ministry. The evidence and our confidence in Him tell us that He will always do what He said He will do.

With this in mind, John 14:12 tells the believer that God will do – we will do the works of Jesus and we will have God answer our prayers.

Most assuredly, I say to you, <u>he who believes in Me</u>, **the works that I do he will do also; and greater *works* than these he will do**, because I go to My Father. And whatever you ask in My name, that I will do, that the Father may be glorified in the Son. **If you ask anything in My name, I will do *it*.** (John 14:12-14 NKJV – emphasis added)

The person who trusts me will not only do what I'm doing but even greater things because I, on my way to the Father, am giving you the same work I've been doing. You can count on it. From now on, whatever you request along the lines of who I am and what I am doing, I'll do it. That's how the Father will be seen for who he is in the Son. I mean it. Whatever you request in this way, I'll do. (John 14:12-14 MSG)

This tells me that we will do the works of Jesus in an obvious and understandable way.

In the NKJV scripture text, the sentence begins with the words *most assuredly.* In other words, Jesus is telling us

- I <u>will</u> do this.
- I am willing and I am able.
- Don't worry, I have finished the work!

- This is a done deal.

He says that we will do His works and in addition to these, even greater works. I always wondered about this statement. What does Jesus mean? *Greater* in verse twelve means more in size or quantity of the preeminent blessings of Gods. There are things that are entirely within His creative majesty. So, we will do the works of Jesus and we will do an even greater quantity.

Jesus was one man that healed many people while He was on the earth. As the number of disciples increased, the disciples healed more and more people. During the ministry of Paul, he brought the good news of Christ to many people. Believers today spread the Gospel and are still bringing many people to Christ.

I have never raised a person from the dead. Does this make this scripture invalid? No. I believe that the miracles did not stop with the passing of the apostles. I am firmly convinced that Jesus Christ is still the same yesterday, today and forever. (Hebrews 13:8) This scripture is found in the context of adopting "strange, new ideas" (v.9 NLT). The existing idea is that Jesus Christ is the same for eternity, and I see this as applying to the continuance of His healing people. The words of Jesus tell us that we would do *greater* works. This is a sure and unshakeable promise. I see the idea of "no miracles today" as denying the words of the Lord Jesus.

In the matter of praying in Jesus name and receiving from God, I use the Bible as my reference for the meaning of asking for <u>anything</u>. I will not ask God to turn me into a giant speckled bird or do things that do not show love. God will meet all of my needs and not give me all of the crazy things I might imagine!

> So I say, let the Holy Spirit guide your lives. Then you won't be doing what your sinful nature craves. The sinful nature wants to do evil, which is the opposite of what the Spirit wants. And the Spirit gives us desires that are the opposite of what the sinful nature desires. These two forces are constantly in opposition to each other, so you are not free to carry out your good intentions. (Galatians 5:16-17 NLT)

I will take the leading of the Holy Spirit to guide me, not the cravings of my earthly self, my flesh. This includes sin (like adultery, murder, theft, etc.) and asking for things that will cause me harm and steer me away from God. One time I asked God for a particular car. He answered "no" because I would ride around in the car and act like I was super-spiritual. "Look at me!" Ouch! However, God was right.

On the other hand, I will not stand in the way of my heavenly Father blessing me. Believers must remember that God blesses us because He loves us. Believers must be ready to help other people – sometimes financially, other times by giving away things that we own. We own our stuff, but our stuff does not own us!

Jesus taught us about our relationship with God, the Holy Spirit. He told us to love Him and obey what He tells us to do. The next thing Jesus tells us is that He is not leaving us as stranded orphans. He will keep us and send the Holy Spirit to help us.

> And I will pray the Father, and He will give you another Helper, that He may abide with you forever - the Spirit of truth, whom the world cannot receive, because it neither sees Him nor knows Him; but you know Him, for He dwells with you and will be in you. I will not leave you orphans; I will come to you. (John 14:16-18 NKJV)

The word *Helper* in verse 16 (*Comforter* in the KJV) is the Greek word *parakletos.* This word means intercessor (one who will plead our case), who will console and help us. In this, we understand that the Holy Spirit will be close to us, and He will go alongside us. When Jesus ascended to Heaven, He told them "Do not leave Jerusalem, but wait for the gift my Father promised." (Acts 1:4b NIV) Jesus promised and the Father sent the Holy Spirit to the followers of Christ.

The Holy Spirit took the place of Jesus here on earth. God the Holy Spirit explained the Gospel and helped the disciples to carry out His orders. Specifically, He gave them power and strength for service and to triumph in Christ when they were persecuted. The Holy Spirit was given to help us to glorify our God. His ministry is to go alongside us and help us, much like when we "yoke up with Jesus."

> Then Jesus said, "Come to me, all of you who are weary and carry heavy burdens, and I will give you rest. Take my yoke upon you. Let me teach you, because I am humble and gentle at heart, and you will find rest for your souls. For my yoke is easy to bear, and the burden I give you is light." (Matthew 11:28-30 NLT)

Being yoked with Jesus is easier because we are not bearing the entire load. With Jesus, He helps us to accomplish His desires and goals. The same is true with the Holy Spirit – He comes up next to us and helps us. We work together with Him (cooperate). We are not independent contractors but are 100% reliant upon Him. Like the relationship between the vine and a branch, we are totally dependent upon Him for our entire life and being, "for without Me you can do nothing." (John 15:5b NKJV)

We tell others that Jesus loves them - Jesus is real and anyone can have a relationship with God because of Jesus. To spread the good news, we are given power by God. We have His authority, motivation and protection to spread the good news.

The Holy Spirit will always testify of Jesus – not some false God. People are entirely wrong when speaking about God the Father and denying that Jesus is God. The enemies of God fight against, dilute or deny the truth of the good news.

This chapter has discussed God the Father, God the Son and God the Holy Spirit. The Trinity is "one God and three persons." Jesus told us that "I and My Father are one." (John 10:30 KJV) Jesus announced to His disciples that the Father would send the Holy Spirit (Acts 1) and then they were suddenly baptized in the Holy Spirit (Acts 2). Again, we see the involvement of Father, Son and Holy Spirit. They were working together in love and lovingly helping people. Believers are an active part of what God has given to His followers over these many years.

Chapter Questions for Discussion or Study

1. Why would unbelievers from other religions see one God and three distinct persons as three gods?

2. How does a believer know that one God and three persons is true?

3. Jesus brought a new covenant. Why is this new covenant better than the old covenant?

4. Several scriptures are listed about a believer's relationship with God. Choose one and why it is an essential part of the believer's life.

5. How does a believer enter a relationship with God the Father? Why is it such a necessary and exciting thing to know the Father?

6. Jesus told the disciples to take Him at His Word. How does someone take God at His Word?

7. What does the word *believe* or *believeth* mean? How is it necessary for the believer to know this?

8. Why is John 12:12-14 so important in a believer's relationship and life with God? What does "greater works" mean to you? How does it apply to your life?

9. What does the word *Helper* mean in John 14:16? How does a believer apply it in their life?

10. A believer should be yoked to Jesus (Matthew 11:28-30). Why is this the best choice for the believer?

11. Why does the Holy Spirit always testify of Jesus?

John 14
Chapter 4
The Way, the Truth And The Life

> Jesus told him, I am the way, the truth, and the life. No one can come to the Father except through me. (John 14:6 NLT)

We see two main points in this scripture.

1. Jesus describes who He is – <u>the</u> way, <u>the</u> truth and <u>the</u> life.
2. He gives information about getting to God the Father.

When Jesus describes who He is, He states that He is <u>the</u> one and only avenue to God and that there are no other ways we can travel to receive a relationship with God.

Again, Jesus describes another exclusive offer from God. He is offering that anyone can get to God the Father through Him. And because it is an exclusive offer, those who want to get to God, can only go through Jesus Christ. Jesus is the way, not a way. There is only one path to God – it's through Jesus Christ.

The word *way* in Greek means a road that is traveled or taking a journey. It is a decision that is made or a way of thinking. This lends itself to determining how we choose to think or how we decide to live our lives. Following "the Way" involves a decision and a plan – "I will follow the Way, I will follow Jesus."

This exclusive offer from God makes Christianity different from the central teachings of Buddhism and Hinduism.

When you travel somewhere in the U.S., there are usually many roads you can drive on to get to your destination. Eastern religions teach that there are many ways to God. It is like the multiple paths that can be traversed to get to the top of the mountain. This tells us they believe that this means that a person can choose from the different ways to reach God or attain enlightenment.

Hindus believe that there are about 33 million Hindu gods. With this many gods, I would have a BIG problem. How in the world would I ever know where to begin? Which god do I trust? Can I be sure that I will receive salvation? Having to deal with many gods confuses me because I am looking for a sure and definite way to get to God.

Because Hinduism teaches that there are many gods, I choose to believe in one God by accepting Jesus Christ as my Lord. I will always put my trust and confidence in Jesus. I choose to accept that He is <u>the</u> way.

The Hindu belief is contrary to what the Bible teaches - there is only one way to God and Jesus is that way.

The "many paths to God" concept does not deal with man's sin problem. Everyone has sinned and does not reach God's standard. (Romans 3:23) That standard is Jesus Christ. How can someone know which path to take on a mountain climb? What if the path results in the hiker falling off a ledge to sure death?

It takes good judgment to choose the correct path when hiking. It takes good spiritual judgment and the leading of the Holy Spirit to reach Jesus. He is the only way to get to God.

> He will be a rich store of salvation, wisdom and knowledge; the fear of the LORD is the key to this treasure. (Isaiah 33:6 NIV)

The fear of the Lord is having a deep reverential respect for Him. This allows us to go to Him and find Him as <u>the</u> way. Jesus is the "key" to our finding God.

> I am the gate; whoever enters through me will be saved. (John 10:9 NIV)

Jesus called Himself the *gate* when He described the means to enter the sheepfold, a walled area where the sheep were kept for protection. Entering the *gate* and approaching God brings salvation. We enter a relationship with God when we go to God through Jesus. He is inviting us to come to Him. We become one of His sheep and become personally involved with Him. We become His friend.

Our society offers a vast number of activities, philosophies and life choices to entertain and guide us. People use these to try to bring meaning to their life. None of these can or will completely satisfy a person. Satisfaction will only come with Jesus in our lives when we accept Him as Lord and Savior.

A relationship with Jesus is the <u>only</u> way for this to happen. This is a clear answer to the question of "how do I find God?" The answer is Jesus. John 14:6 is a promise from God made personally to you – Jesus is the way.

Because Jesus is <u>the</u> Truth, He is absolutely dependable.

> God did this so that, by two unchangeable things in which it is impossible for God to lie, we who have fled to take hold of the hope set before us may be greatly encouraged. (Hebrews 6:18 NIV)

God makes promises and always keeps them. We know that what He says is true. His character is truth, He speaks true things and He can be trusted.

Believers are not slaves to lying and other sins. Believers are made new creatures in Christ and set free from sin.

> So if the Son sets you free, you will be free indeed. (John 8:36 NIV)

> Sin is no longer your master, for you no longer live under the requirements of the law. Instead, you live under the freedom of God's grace. (Romans 6:14 NLT)

The KJV states that "sin shall not have dominion over you." Jesus releases us from the need to lie because we now live in His truth. If lying is a sin that tempts you, learn to live in His freedom. Make the decision to tell the truth each time you have an opportunity to lie. This freedom from the sin of lying is available to you.

When a person testifies in court, it is expected that the testimony that is given is "the whole truth and nothing but the truth." Likewise, parents and teachers desire that they get accurate and factual information. A police officer hopes that he is being told what really happened when he is conducting an investigation. We want the truth, but we don't always get it in society.

People are not always "truth-tellers." But Jesus is different. He is always true. He is the Truth.

> Let God be found true [as He will be], though every person *be found* a liar, just as it is written [in Scripture] (Romans 3:4a AMP)

People can tell lies, will tell lies, and do tell lies when they are confronted with the truth. The verse in Romans tells us that God is always true. We can live the truth of Jesus Christ when we trust and follow God. We become the righteousness of God in Christ and this changes us.

People do not have to be taught to lie. This is evident with young children. Lying happens in some of the craziest ways! We often hear "No. I didn't take a cookie." "He started it!" "I don't know who did it."

Only when a person surrenders their life to Jesus Christ can they find the Truth in Him. New believers learn the Truth from the Word of God, renew their old minds to new godly thinking and develop a relationship with God through Jesus Christ.

Jesus is <u>the</u> Life. Like the exclusive nature of the Way and the Truth, Jesus is the <u>only</u> real Life. We talk about life in relation to the different things we do, to having good health, the way we live and other things. *Life* in this context is the Greek word *zoe*. John 3:16 says that Jesus gives us *zoe* – eternal life.

> For God so loved the world that he gave his one and only Son, that whoever believes in him shall not perish but have eternal life. For God did not send his Son into the world to condemn the world, but to save the world through him. (John 3:16-17 NIV)

Zoe means the fulness of a life which belongs to God. This is a life where someone is devoted to God and puts their trust in Christ. In John 3:16, *zoe* is coupled with another word, making it *eternal* life with God. So here, we learn about a complete and extraordinary life where a believer lives in Christ and is kept by Him for eternity.

> That, however, is not the way of life you learned when you heard about Christ and were taught in him in accordance with the <u>truth</u> that is in Jesus. You were taught, with regard to your former way of life, to put off your old self, which is being corrupted by its deceitful desires; to be made new in the attitude of your minds; and to put on the new self, created to be like God in true righteousness and holiness. (Ephesians 4:20-24 NIV, underline added)

The eternal life we receive is true – God did it. Regardless of people rejecting God as they resist and insult God with their spiritual ignorance, eternal life is true. Believers are taught to quit the old life and start new by clothing ourselves in our new life. "The old is gone and the new is come." (2 Corinthians 5:17) Believers are recreated to be like God – to live a life of righteousness and holiness.

Believers learn from the Bible about the character of God as a regular part of growing in their new life in Christ. The older believers in the Church are responsible to teach the younger believers. Learning God's truths in the Bible becomes a new way of life for the Christian.

Followers of Jesus learn to pray using "the name of Jesus." These are not "magic words" to help the prayer or a prewritten religious formula. This is using the authority of Jesus when we pray in His name.

In closing, the goal of religion is to get to God. Christianity provides the only Way.

Chapter Questions for Discussion or Study

1. Why is Jesus the only way to God?

2. Explain how "one way to God" differs from "many ways to God." Why is "one way to God" a better "path?"

3. Believers are free from having to sin. Why is this an essential part of life as a believer?

4. Explain why people lie and how a believer can be free from lying?

5. When did you first become aware of your freedom from sin?

6. How is the Greek word *zoe* translated in English? What does *zoe* mean for the believer in Jesus Christ?

7. When and how does someone receive eternal life? Why does eternal life begin when we are saved and not just when we die and go to heaven?

8. Why do believers pray and use the name of Jesus?

John 14
Chapter 5
The Comforter

We discussed the Heavenly Father, the Son of God and the Holy Spirit in chapter three. The Holy Spirit is called Comforter, Advocate, Helper, Friend and Spirit of Truth in the Scriptures. These are the English words used to translate His name from the original Greek scriptures. His name is *parakletos* in Greek.

I think the most straightforward definition for *parakletos* is *one who comes alongside*. Think about the times that you help someone. You come up alongside them and ask "can I help you?" Maybe you are helping a person carry a table – you have joined your efforts to complete the task and move the table. If your child needs help with their school work, you sit next to them and help solve the math problem or write a paragraph. These are all actions that speak of coming alongside someone and helping them.

The Holy Spirit comes alongside and helps us in a much more excellent way. He brings solutions to challenges and problems, helps us resolve family issues and complete the work that God has given us. These are only a few ways that the Holy Spirit helps us. Because the Holy Spirit is God, He is all-powerful (omnipotent), knows everything (omniscient) and He is everywhere (omnipresent). And on top of this, He is Love. (1 John 4:16) This is the Holy Spirit and He is the one who is helping us.

God sent the Holy Spirit to fill the believers on the day of Pentecost. He came alongside them and helped them.

> When the day of Pentecost came, they were all together in one place. Suddenly a sound like the blowing of a violent wind came from heaven and filled the whole house where they were sitting. They saw what seemed to be tongues of fire that separated and came to rest on each of them. All of them were filled with the Holy Spirit and began to speak in other tongues as the Spirit enabled them. (Acts 2:1-4 NIV)

They were together praying. When the Holy Spirit filled them, there was a loud noise that caused a crowd to gather in the street. Peter stepped forward and preached the good news of Jesus Christ to the crowd. The NLT says that Peter shouted to the people – it was a

HUGE crowd and he knew they needed to hear His message.

> "So let everyone in Israel know for certain that God has made this Jesus, whom you crucified, to be both Lord and Messiah!" Peter's words pierced their hearts, and they said to him and to the other apostles, "Brothers, what should we do?" Peter replied, "Each of you must repent of your sins and turn to God, and be baptized in the name of Jesus Christ for the forgiveness of your sins. Then you will receive the gift of the Holy Spirit. This promise is to you, to your children, and to those far away - all who have been called by the Lord our God." Then Peter continued preaching for a long time, strongly urging all his listeners, "Save yourselves from this crooked generation!" Those who believed what Peter said were baptized and added to the church that day— about 3,000 in all. (Acts 2:36-41 NLT)

Peter preached the good news to the people in the street. The Holy Spirit moved upon them and they committed their lives to Christ. That day in Jerusalem, about 3,000 people were saved. This is a perfect example of God the Holy Spirit coming alongside people who desperately needed God in their lives. It was the Holy Spirit that helped them to receive Christ.

All of this happened because of what Jesus said.

> Once when He was eating with them, He commanded them, "Do not leave Jerusalem until the Father sends you the gift He promised, as I told you before. John baptized with water, but in just a few days you will be baptized with the Holy Spirit." (Acts 1:4-5 NLT)

There are two main things in this verse. One is, to wait for the Father to send the Holy Spirit. The other is God will b<u>aptize</u> you with the Holy Spirit. We see this happening with the disciples in Acts 2. They obeyed Him by waiting. God filled them with His Holy Spirit.

Baptized means to immerse and overwhelm. Those disciples who were waiting for God were immersed as if someone tossed them into a swimming pool. It was such a new experience for them and the presence of God was so real, so vital and <u>they</u> were a part of the Holy Spirit coming. They were overwhelmed.

Overwhelm is a word that means *to entirely cover or submerge*. When a person is baptized in water, they are "overwhelmed" by the water. The disciples were *"overwhelmed"* when the

Holy Spirit came on them, to the degree that they were completely filled up with God. The Holy Spirit accomplished His mission when He filled them like a container full of water.

> God poured out His Holy Spirit that day. The disciples spoke in tongues. The miracle of the tongues from the Holy Spirit is that the people said that they heard them "speaking in our own tongues the wonderful works of God." (Acts 2:11b NKJV) Some of the people that gathered thought the disciples were drunk, but Peter straightened them out. He preached the inspired Word of God and the people were "cut to the heart." (Acts 2:37 NKJV)
>
> Peter talked to them at length and told them to seek God. "Get out while you can; get out of this sick and stupid culture!" (Acts 2:40 MSG)

This filling by the Holy Spirit points the believer to the person of Jesus Christ. The Holy Spirit always glorifies Christ and the work He does among people. Speaking of the Holy Spirit

> He will glorify Me, for He will take of what is Mine and declare *it* to you. All things that the Father has are Mine. Therefore I said that He will take of Mine

and declare *it* to you. (John 16:14-15 NKJV)

All that belongs to the Father is mine; this is why I said, 'The Spirit will tell you whatever he receives from me. (John 16:14-15 NLT)

Charles Spurgeon, a very well-known preacher from London in the 1800s was preaching about the Holy Spirit and said the following.

> "It is the Chief office of the Holy Spirit to glorify Christ. He does many things, but this is what he aims at in all of them, to glorify Christ. Brethren, what the Holy Ghost does must be right for us to imitate: therefore, let us endeavor to glorify Christ. To what higher ends can we devote ourselves than to something to which God the Holy Ghost devotes himself? Be this, then, your emotional prayer, 'Blessed Spirit, help me ever to glorify the Lord Jesus Christ!'" (Charles Spurgeon, July 26, 1888, Volume 40)

The Holy Spirit glorifies Christ, and this is the subject that Peter spoke to the street crowd on Pentecost. Peter pointed the people to forsake their failing, wicked lives and hear about Christ - "Get out while you can; get out of this sick and stupid culture!" Believers rely today on the Holy Spirit. As we preach, teach and share the

Word of God, we lead people to Christ and bring glory to Him. All of this is inspired and directed by God the Holy Spirit.

The Holy Spirit was involved with the creation of the world. In Genesis 1, the Holy Spirit was over the water, ready to move. God spoke, and the Spirit moved and created the world. We see the Holy Spirit and God the Father speaking the Word of God in creation. God's power came together that day in the three persons of God.

In John 1, the scripture sheds more light on the creation and the ministry of Jesus Christ.

> In the beginning was the Word, and the Word was with God, and the Word was God. He was with God in the beginning. Through him all things were made; without him nothing was made that has been made. In him was life, and that life was the light of all mankind. The light shines in the darkness, and the darkness has not overcome it. (John 1:1-5 NIV)

God spoke precisely what He wanted with His Word and brought about the creation. The Spirit created as He heard the Word of God. He waited and followed the Word of God exactly.

The Holy Spirit is our teacher.

> But when the Father sends the Advocate as my representative - that is, the Holy Spirit - he will teach you everything and will remind you of everything I have told you. (John 14:26 NLT)

> But the Helper (Comforter, Advocate, Intercessor - Counselor, Strengthener, Standby), the Holy Spirit, whom the Father will send in My name [in My place, to represent Me and act on My behalf], He will teach you all things. And He will help you remember everything that I have told you. (John 14:26 AMP)

The Holy Spirit will teach us and reteach us all about Jesus. Remember that Jesus came to give us the good news that God's not mad and He wants us to come home to Him. Like the prodigal son who left his father and his home, God wants us to return to Him. Whether it is becoming saved or dealing with sin in our life, God wants us home and restored to Him. This is the Gospel, the Good News from God through Jesus Christ.

A teacher is someone who brings and conveys information and ideas to you. They direct your learning. Take a look at this description of a teacher's duties.

The primary role of a teacher is to deliver classroom instruction that helps students learn. To accomplish this, teachers must prepare effective lessons, grade student work and offer encouragement, manage classroom materials, productively navigate the curriculum, and collaborate with other staff. (www.thoughtco.com)

When we consider the responsibilities of a teacher, we consider how the Holy Spirit is <u>our</u> Teacher.

<u>He delivers instruction</u> as He tells us about God and how we serve God. The Teacher gave Peter the words to preach to bring people to Christ on the day of Pentecost. (Acts 2)

<u>He prepares effective lessons</u> for us to use. The Holy Spirit creates and tailors individual experiences that allow us to grow and mature in God. We read and hear the Word of God, we follow God and we are involved with people and situations that help us and them to grow and change. Believers become more like Christ.

<u>He gives feedback</u> telling us how we are doing. The Holy Spirit guided Paul and the people with him while they were on a missionary journey. He told them to go and not to go to certain places.

> Paul and his companions traveled throughout the region of Phrygia and Galatia, having been kept by the Holy Spirit from preaching the word in the province of Asia. When they came to the border of Mysia, they tried to enter Bithynia, but the Spirit of Jesus would not allow them to. So they passed by Mysia and went down to Troas. During the night Paul had a vision of a man of Macedonia standing and begging him, "Come over to Macedonia and help us." After Paul had seen the vision, we got ready at once to leave for Macedonia, concluding that God had called us to preach the gospel to them. (Acts 16:6-10 NIV)

The leading and guiding of the Holy Spirit are seen in the work of Paul and those who were with him. Paul knew when he obeyed and did the right thing and pleased God.

<u>He manages classroom materials</u>. In our service to God, He meets all of our needs in agreement with His riches in glory. (Philippians 4:19) This scripture was written within the context of generous believers. In this Paul is telling us that God is very generous to His children. Believers know that as we give "it shall be given unto us." (Luke 6:38) As a school principal authorizes the purchase of

needed classroom materials, so God provides for all of our needs. We serve a good God who loves His people.

<u>He navigates us through the curriculum</u>. It has been said, "Read the Bible, know the truth." The Holy Spirit guides us and illuminates the Scriptures making them alive. The Bible is our curriculum and the Holy Spirit is our Teacher. We learn it and then we share it with others. The Church was sent by Jesus to go to everyone everywhere and bring them the Gospel. Paul did this through the leading and the power of the Holy Spirit. As we follow the Holy Spirit, we teach His curriculum using His book the Bible.

> All Scripture is God-breathed and is useful for **teaching**, rebuking, correcting and **training in righteousness**, so that the **servant of God may be thoroughly equipped** for every good work. (2 Timothy 3:16-17 NIV, emphasis added)

<u>He helps us collaborate with other staff</u>. Just as school teachers have a unity of purpose and work towards a common set of goals, so it is with believers. Paul encouraged the church in Ephesus to join together in God's peace. We cooperate because we are His Body and work under the Holy Spirit's direction.

> Make every effort to keep yourselves united in the Spirit, binding yourselves together with peace. For there is one body and one Spirit, just as you have been called to one glorious hope for the future. (Ephesian 4:3-4 NLT)

Believers follow <u>our</u> Teacher, the Holy Spirit and learn from Him. We go where He sends us and carry out the tasks He gives to each of us. As we obey Him, we are blessed. In all of this, the Gospel is preached, lives are changed and God is glorified.

> Don't you realize that all of you together are the temple of God and that the Spirit of God lives in you? (1 Corinthians 3:16 NLT)

This scripture reminds us that God is holy and as we work with Him, we are involved in the holy work of God. Because our bodies are the temple of the Holy Spirit, we must use judgment in the things that we choose to become involved in and in our personal behavior.

All of the world's unbelievers will not accept God the Holy Spirit, because they don't believe in God. That's where the unbelief comes in – without believing and accepting Christ, a person cannot truly know God.

> The world cannot accept him, because it neither sees him nor knows him. But you know him, for he lives with you and will be in you. (John 14:17 NIV)

> whom the world cannot receive [and take to its heart] because it does not see Him or know Him, *but* you know Him because He (the Holy Spirit) remains with you *continually* and will be in you. (John 14:17 AMP)

Christians are different. We follow and obey an invisible God. We love Him and receive Him as Lord and Savior. Our relationship with God is a sure thing!

We see Him, know Him and allow Him into our lives – this is our relationship with God. This is because we believe in Christ and have been made righteous by Jesus Christ.

After Jesus left the earth, He went to be with the Father. He sent the Holy Spirit, who will always be with us and live in us.

> But the Helper (Comforter, Advocate, Intercessor—Counselor, Strengthener, Standby), the Holy Spirit, whom the Father will send in My name [in My place, to represent Me and act on My behalf], He will teach you all things. And

> He will help you remember everything that I have told you. (John 14:26 AMP)
>
> While being together *and* eating with them, He commanded them not to leave Jerusalem, but to wait for what the Father had promised, "Of which," *He said*, "you have heard Me speak. For John baptized with water, but you will be baptized *and* empowered *and* united with the Holy Spirit, not long from now." (Acts 1:4-5 AMP)

God sent the Holy Spirit to His Body, the Church. We see the Holy Spirit in the lives of the disciples. The book of Acts shows that the disciples and followers of Jesus people were clearly changed. The disciples preached the Word of God, they healed the sick, raised the dead and lead the Church with God's authority. Even though Jesus was physically gone, God was still with them daily. *Parakletos* was with them and He is with us now.

The Church is the embodiment of Jesus Christ on earth – <u>we</u> are <u>His Body</u>. As believers live and follow His will, we are powered by the Holy Spirit. This is how believers can carry the Gospel to the entire world. This is how the disciples performed miracles and why the church is still involved with doing miracles today. The Holy Spirit filling believers is why they were able to do the works that Jesus did. Believers are charged and empowered to do what He did, and even greater things – bring the Word, love people and perform miracles. The ministry of Jesus is active in the Church today. He still heals, raises the dead and baptizes believers with the Holy Spirit.

The Church carries the love of God to those within the Church and those outside the Church - the family of God and an unbelieving society.

> Each of you should use whatever gift you have received to serve others, as faithful stewards of God's grace in its various forms. If anyone speaks, they should do so as one who speaks the very words of God. If anyone serves, they should do so with the strength God provides so that in all things God may be praised through Jesus Christ. To him be the glory and the power forever and ever. Amen. (1 Peter 4:10-11 NIV)

> This is how we know what love is: Jesus Christ laid down his life for us. And we ought to lay down our lives for our brothers and sisters. If anyone has material possessions and sees a brother or sister in need but has no pity on them, how can the love of God be in that

person? Dear children, let us not love with words or speech but with actions and in truth. (1 John 3:16-18 NIV)

Believers love people as God loved the world. His love for people is given to us by God and we love people by His power. Believers love people because He is in us.

The early disciples loved people and today's disciples love people. God loved the world and sent Jesus and believers love the world and carry the Gospel to people everywhere. This is the mission of the Church – bring God's love to needful people and share the Word of God to bring salvation. The Church is called to love the important and unimportant and reach people who are seemingly unlovable people. These are the people the Church is called and commanded to love. We love and help and love them. This is the love of God in action!

There are many ways that the Holy Spirit helps the Church – God's multi-faceted ministry to the earth.

- He is our Teacher – John 14:26
- He testifies of Jesus – John 15:26
- He testifies that we are children of our Father – Romans 8:14-17
- He guarantees our eternal bodies in God's presence – 2 Corinthians 5:5

- He is the promise of His inheritance – Ephesians 1:14
- He brings God's wisdom and revelation – Ephesians 1:17
- He is the gift that the Father promised – Acts 1:4
- He baptizes and fills the people of the Church – Acts 1:5, Acts 2:4
- He gives believers the power of God – Acts 1:8
- He sends the Church with power to witness to everyone about Jesus – Acts 1:8
- He brings the thoughts of God to believers – 1 Corinthians 2:11
- He is everywhere and with us (omnipresent) – Psalm 139:7-12
- He knows everything (omniscient) – 1 Corinthians 2:10-16
- He is all-powerful (omnipotent) – Acts 1:8
- He tells us we are God's own children and heirs – Galatians 4:6-7
- He will guide us into all truth – John 16:13

What more can we say about the Holy Spirit? He is great and He brings God's love to us and for us. He empowers the Church to bring the

Gospel to all the people in the world. All of this is because He is a loving God.

> "'Come, Holy Spirit' has been called the most essential prayer of the Church. So, together with all God's Church, we pray 'Come, Holy Spirit!' for the sake of the Gospel, for our lives and the lives of those we touch, and for the life of the world." (Vineyardusa.org)

Come Holy Spirit.

Chapter Questions for Discussion or Study

1. What is the Greek language name of the Holy Spirit?

2. Describe a time when the Holy Spirit came alongside you and helped you? What was your reaction to God's help?

3. As a believer, when have you come alongside someone and helped them?

4. What did Peter preach to the crowd in the street on the Day of Pentecost? What happened? How was God honored and glorified?

5. What is the literal meaning of the word *baptism*? Why is this a good word when describing water baptism or the baptism of the Holy Spirit?

6. Peter told the crowd to leave their lives and turn to Christ. Why is this relevant in today's culture?

7. The Holy Spirit is our Teacher. Write one or two ways that He teaches you about following God.

8. We discussed the "Role of the Teacher." Write two of the responsibilities of God the Holy Spirit, our Teacher.

9. How are believers different from unbelievers? How have you seen this difference in your life?

10. Believers are the Body of Christ on this earth. Describe one way that you are aware of His Body on the earth.

11. God loves all people. How does a believer express and give people the love of God?

12. What is the mission of all believers?

13. List three of the ways that the Holy Spirit helps the Church serve God. How have you seen the Holy Spirit help you?

14. Fill in the sentence.

>This filling by the _____ _____ points the believer to the person of _____ _____.

John 14
Chapter 6
A Man Of God

Warren Wiersbe was a man of God who is now in heaven with Jesus. There is a wonderfully written short biography about him on the Moody Bible Institute web page (moodybible.org). He glorified God while serving the Body of Christ. He is someone who provided a good Christian role model in his life. We lead and follow others in the Body of Christ. People like Warren Wiersbe inspire and encourage me to follow and serve God.

Hebrews 11 discusses several people who are great examples to follow. We don't worship these people as a special class of "God-people" because they are the people of God just like we are. They are simply believers who trusted God. These people are godly examples who provide general guidelines for effectively following God. It makes sense to look to and learn from righteous people who love God and sincerely serve Him. These are Christian role models.

These godly people were just like you and me. They took the challenges in their life, trusted God and actively lived what Jesus said to do, "Have faith in God." (Mark 11:22 NIV) I have examples who are role models at my church – my pastors, Richard and Christine Dunk. I have friends in the ministry who are examples to follow as they serve God – missionaries and preachers to the world Fred and Debbie Davis. I have a best friend who is an example of God's love, someone who serves God together with me – my wife, Sarah. I learn from the godly things that these people do and follow God together with them. These people and those in Hebrews 11 that God sent as examples that God sent. Follow God and learn from these people.

By one account, Warren Wiersbe wrote over 150 books about theology and serving God. I own both of the Wiersbe Bible Commentaries (OT and NT), which are published by David C. Cook (and widely available). I don't say this as an advertisement for the books, but rather to say that they are well-written and beneficial for study. Believers are told to study the Word of God to bring God's approval to their lives and ministry. Books like Wiersbe's meet this standard of study.

Wiersbe wrote some significant observations about John 14 (p.279-283). He wrote six statements about John 14 that provide an excellent way to look at this chapter. John 14 shows Jesus speaking to His disciples and sharing many things. He told them He was going away, but that they knew God and everything would be okay. The Father would care for them as Jesus had cared for them. Today, His care for us is sure and we can have confidence in Him.

In his New Testament commentary, Wiersbe wrote these truths from John 14.

1. We are going to Heaven.
2. You know the Father right now.
3. You have the privilege of prayer.
4. We have the Holy Spirit.
5. We enjoy the Father's love.
6. We have His gift of peace.

(Warren Wiersbe, *Wiersbe Bible Commentary NT*, 2007)

These six statements provide a framework to consider and help us understand what Jesus told us in John 14. This framework can help you organize your thinking as you study.

I would add the following to Wiersbe's list of statements

1. Jesus told us that He would go to the Father and make a permanent and eternal place for us.

   There is more than enough room in my Father's home. If this were not so, would I have told you that I am going to prepare a place for you? When everything is ready, I will come and get you, so that you will always be with me where I am. (John 14:2-3 NLT)

   Heaven is our sure eternal destination. I believe this with all my heart – I will be going to Heaven to be with Jesus. Some people say that we can lose our salvation, that our behavior can be so sinful and spiritually atrocious that we backslide into unbelief and become completely separated from God. I have issues with this viewpoint because Jesus said God will never leave or abandon us.

   Be strong and courageous. Do not be afraid or terrified because of them, for the LORD your God goes with you; he will never leave you nor forsake you." (Deuteronomy 31:6 NIV)

Let your character [your moral essence, your inner nature] be free from the love of money [shun greed—be financially ethical], being content with what you have; for He has said, "I WILL NEVER [under any circumstances] DESERT YOU [nor give you up nor leave you without support, nor will I in any degree leave you helpless], NOR WILL I FORSAKE or LET YOU DOWN or RELAX MY HOLD ON YOU [assuredly not]!" (Hebrews 13:5 AMP)

These verses are given to righteous believers – those who have received Jesus as Lord. God calls every follower of Christ to submit their lives to God and resist wickedness, specifically to "resist the devil and He will run away." (James 4:6 NIV) Believers are called to love God not to love money and possessions. Loving money and possessions is a false love and the root of all evil. It causes us to wander away from God and experience heartbreak. (1 Timothy 6:10 NLT) This does not talk about God rejecting and pushing us away, He is simply telling us to trust God/resist evil and love God/not love money.

Some believers choose to abuse this eternal salvation from God. They use the concept of "once saved always saved" to sin without control. Paul asks

Are you so foolish? After beginning by means of the Spirit, are you now trying to finish by means of the flesh? (Galatians 3:3 NIV)

Believers were saved through the work of the Holy Spirit and believers must live their daily lives in the power of God the Holy Spirit. We looked at the verses above that told us to resist the devil and wickedness and to love God not money. The Bible is very clear about living righteously and not committing sin. Christians are to live according to the Spirit of God, not give in to the temptations to our flesh.

"Once saved" inspires us to live saved. We see people in our lives and in the Bible who are examples. Believers should resist the bad examples that are a real part of our society – loving money and accumulating possessions, hating people, openly sinning, ignoring God, embracing man-centered humanism, living life as if they are a god, etc.

For you are free, yet you are God's slaves, so don't use your freedom as an excuse to do evil. (1 Timothy 2:16 NLT)

I am a saved individual. I am going to trust God to help me live for Him.

But God is my helper. The Lord keeps me alive! For you have rescued me from my troubles and helped me to triumph over my enemies. (Psalm 54:4,7)
Psalm 54 deals with BIG problems in David's life.
We are going to heaven to live with Jesus for eternity. Let's live like we are heaven-bound!

2. <u>You know the Father right now</u>.
   The disciples knew Jesus. They lived day-by-day with Him and saw Him

worship and love the Father. Jesus told them that they have seen the Father.

Jesus said to him, "Have I been with you so long, and yet you have not known Me, Philip? He who has seen Me has seen the Father; so how can you say, 'Show us the Father'? Do you not believe that I am in the Father, and the Father in Me? The words that I speak to you I do not speak on My own *authority*, but the Father who dwells in Me does the works. Believe Me that I *am* in the Father and the Father in Me, or else believe Me for the sake of the works themselves. (John 14:9-11 NKJV)

Like the heading, Jesus tells us today, "You know the Father right now." Sure, we have been made righteous when we received Jesus as Lord and Savior. However, this verse tells us that we must believe that the Father and Jesus are one. This verse tells that Jesus speaks to people through the Father's authority. This verse tells us that "I *am* in the Father and the Father in

Me" and that the miracles and works of Jesus bring us to believe in Him.

Today, we know Jesus. We see Him and grow in Him as we pray, read the Bible and fellowship with other believers. He knows us right down to the thoughts, ideas and plans that we make.

Oh yes, you shaped me first inside, then out; you formed me in my mother's womb. I thank you, High God - you're breathtaking! Body and soul, I am marvelously made! I worship in adoration—what a creation! You know me inside and out, you know every bone in my body; You know exactly how I was made, bit by bit, how I was sculpted from nothing into something. Like an open book, you watched me grow from conception to birth; all the stages of my life were spread out before you, The days of my life all prepared before I'd even lived one day. (Psalm 139:13-16 MSG)

What a wonderful thing – we know God and He knows us. His love is given to us and we love Him because He first loved us. (1 John 4:18-19 NLT) Every believer is loved.

3. <u>We have the privilege of prayer</u>. Jesus makes it very clear that we should fervently and diligently seek God. Jesus actually invites us to talk to God as we pray to Him.

Ask and it will be given to you; seek and you will find; knock and the door will be opened to you. For everyone who asks receives; the one who seeks finds; and to the one who knocks, the door will be opened. (Matthew 7:7-8 NIV)

Jesus talked to God and believers talk to God. We actually have a constant and ongoing conversation with God as we pray without stopping. This connection with God makes us rich, way beyond extreme financial wealth or a luxury beachfront mansion in Malibu! I talk with God and am joined with Him!

God speaks with us and we speak with Him. He listens, we listen. He acts and we act as we obey Him.

This is the privilege of prayer in action.

Prayer is a relationship, not just words spoken. I was raised in church to pray using the Lord's Prayer. (Matthew 6:9-13) The call to prayer was always followed by the people saying "Our father who art in Heaven..." This prayer is sacred because it is in the Scriptures.

Prayer is more than a generous benefit or something really good. It is spending time with God. We have a relationship with Him. People who have a relationship relate to each other, laugh openly, walk together and talk together.

Noah and Enoch walked with God. Abraham was a friend of God. Believers are friends with God through Jesus. This is the blessing of the wonderful relationship with God.

I no longer call you servants, because a servant does not know his master's business. Instead, I have called you friends, for everything that I learned from my Father I have made known to you. (John 15:15 NIV)

The word *friend* is based on the Greek word *philos* from where we get the concept of friendship and brotherly love. A friend wishes a friend well – "have a GREAT day!" and really means it from the heart. Friends are our companions and those we associate with our friends. I pray that God will bless my friends. All of this tells us that we are friends with God.

An old hymn *What a Friend We Have in Jesus* was written in 1855. It is so encouraging that it draws the believer to pray and draw closer to God.

> What a friend we have in Jesus
> All our sins and griefs to bear
> And what a privilege to carry
> Everything to God in prayer

Our friend Jesus wants us to pray to Him about everything – take "everything to the Lord in prayer."

Don't worry about <u>anything</u>; instead, pray about <u>everything</u>. Tell God what you need, and thank him for all he has done. (Philippians 4:6 NLT, underlining added)

Take it to the Lord in prayer.

1. <u>We have the Holy Spirit</u>.
   We discussed the Holy Spirit, the Comforter in Chapter 5. Comforter is only one of the many character qualities that are shown in the Scriptures. The Holy Spirit is the Teacher of the Church. He is the one who testifies about Jesus. He is the Spirit of Truth.

   We are sealed with the Holy Spirit. This seal is His guarantee that we are His people.

   In Him you also *trusted,* after you heard the word of truth, the gospel of your salvation; in whom also, having believed, you were sealed with the Holy Spirit of promise, who is the guarantee of our inheritance until the redemption of the purchased possession, to the praise of His glory. (Ephesians 1:13-14 NKJV)

And now you Gentiles have also heard the truth, the Good News that God saves you. And when you believed in Christ, he identified you as his own by giving you the Holy Spirit, whom he promised long ago. The Spirit is God's guarantee that he will give us the inheritance he promised and that he has purchased us to be his own people. He did this so we would praise and glorify him. (Ephesians 1:13-14 NLT)

This *seal* from God (translated as *guarantee* in the NLT) is similar to the wax seal put on old documents to certify the document officially. The seal told people that "this document is genuine." In today's society, our signature is our seal. When we sign a contract, we say we will fulfill what is specified. God's seal is a mark upon us and guarantees to the world that we are authentic and belong to God. He seals and promises that He redeems us <u>now</u> and that we will be with Him for <u>eternity</u>.

We are sealed with God's Holy Spirit. He guarantees our salvation.

God Himself seals us. This eternal presence of God is Him with us. He saved us, He fills us and lives with us and within us forever. We are His children and those who love Him.

2. <u>We enjoy the Father's love</u>.
God sent Jesus to the earth to redeem mankind. This showed God's *greater* love. We have redemption from God because of this love. (John 3:16-17)

My command is this: Love each other as I have loved you. Greater love has no one than this: to lay down one's life for one's friends. (John 15:12-13 NIV)

The Greek word for *greater* is *megas*. His *megas* love is numerous, large and abundant. This tells us that God <u>has</u> BIG LOVE, because God <u>is</u> love. (1 John 4:8) God's love is perfect, infinite and sure.

The love that the Father has given to us changes our lives.

Behold what manner of love the Father has bestowed on us, that we should be called children of God! Therefore the world does not know us, because it did not know Him. Beloved, now we are children of God; and it has not yet been revealed what we shall be, but we know that when He is revealed, we shall be like Him, for we shall see Him as He is. And everyone who has this hope in Him purifies himself, just as He is pure. (1 John 3:1-3 NKJV)

We are the loved children of God. We see God's act of love in the crucifixion and resurrection of Jesus. The Father sent Him to die so He could redeem us from sin and give us new life. With all of this, He brought us into His family as sons and daughters, not orphans. We are the permanent children of God. We are His children forever.

3. <u>We have His gift of peace</u>.
   Jesus gave us a priceless gift – He personally provides His peace to us.

   Peace I leave with you, My peace I give to you; not as the world gives do I give to you. Let not your heart be

troubled, neither let it be afraid. (John 14:27 NKJV)
I am leaving you with a gift—peace of mind and heart. And the peace I give is a gift the world cannot give. So don't be troubled or afraid. (John 14:27 NLT)

The Prince of Peace brings the new life of salvation to us. Believers enter the peace of God when they enter the new life of salvation. God's peace is more than the "absence of war," as we see *peace* defined in our society. It is peace with God that we receive from Christ. We are no longer afraid of God. Believers personally experience His love and know our lives have been changed. We now have a deep respect for God and are thankful.

Peace is the state of God's presence where someone is sure of their salvation and knows contentment because God is in control of their life.

And the peace of God, which transcends all understanding, will guard your hearts and your minds in Christ Jesus. (Philippians 4:7 NIV)

The context of Philippians 4:7 tells us several things. First, we should live a life of rejoicing in God – always being extraordinarily thankful and glad for what God has done for us. When we rejoice, we tell others about how God has worked in our life. Second, the KJV of the Bible states that our *moderation* should be apparent to everyone – this is our fairness and our dealing with people. We show God at work in our lives when we are kind and gentle. Harsh people come across as mean. Kind and gentle people are those who respect and care for others. Third, do not worry and be full of anxiety. Rather, ask and thank God when you tell Him about your needs. When we do this as a part of our relationship with Him, we will actively experience peace. Our life is one with God through Jesus Christ and His peace will occur naturally. We live with God, we love God and His ways change us – we will be at peace.

God's peace is something that unbelievers cannot understand

because they don't know God. Some unbelievers deny His peace and everything about God. They say that He doesn't exist and isn't real. To them, God is just a "make-believe" manufactured fable for children or He is a frail old man who just doesn't care. These things are big lies about God. Unbelievers just go on with their lives without God's presence and personal intervention.

The peace of God makes absolute spiritual sense to believers. When God fills your life, His peace is to be expected and absolutely normal. Believers encounter massive problems in their lives that are like the huge storm that pounded against the house built on a rock. (Matthew 7:24-27) Like the house, believers thrive and survive these "storms." It is only the peace of God that comes from His presence that allows the confidence. His Holy Spirit, His Word and His presence bring His peace. God's peace defies logic to the people of the world. However, believers see His peace and say "thank you Lord."

Blessed are the peacemakers, for they will be called children of God. (Matthew 5:9 NIV)

God blesses those who work for peace, for they will be called the children of God. (Matthews 5:9 NLT)

We bring God's peace to people and we live the peace that God gives even though we are in this ungodly world.

We are the children of our Father. We love peace because of God in our lives. I believe that peacemakers are those who love God and do the work of God by carrying Jesus Christ to people. We can stop wars and eliminate nuclear weapons, but until a person receives Christ, they will never know peace. Jesus gives us His peace one person at a time. Peacemakers bring His peace through the Word of God, prayer, preaching and sharing Jesus Christ with individuals.

Believers have the presence of God in their lives. This allows us to be positive to believers and unbelievers. As we live for God, we grow and mature in His ways. This is when we are able to serve as positive role models for Christ.

We see this godliness in the life of Warren Wiersbe and in the way he affected and influenced so many people for the Lord Jesus Christ.

Live for Christ and be a positive role model today. You will never know all of the people you affect for the Gospel of Jesus Christ.

Know God, serve God and help others find and know God.

Chapter Questions for Discussion or Study

1. Why does God send "role models" to the Body of Christ for believers to learn from?

2. Identify one person who has been a role model in your life.

3. After reading 2 Timothy 2:15, describe why we study and why it is the desire of God in our lives.

4. In what way do you find prayer a privilege?

5. Identify someone in the Bible who was a friend of God and walked with God. What positive characteristics help you understand a relationship with God?

6. Describe your friendship and walk with God. In what areas do you see victory and where do you see challenges?

7. What things are important to be taken to God in prayer? Why?

8. Describe your awareness of the Holy Spirit in your life and the lives of other believers. How have you seen the Holy Spirit's presence?

9. How have you experienced God's peace in your life?

10. Fill in the blank.

    God's peace is a _____ from God.

John 14
Chapter 7
Obey His Commands

Jesus tells us in John 14:15 that our obedience demonstrates our love for Him.

> If you love me, keep my commands. (John 14:15 NIV)

> If you love me, show it by doing what I've told you. (John 14:15 MSG)

The Scriptures make it clear that obedience to God is better than the ritual of sacrifice and complies with God's wishes for us. The sacrifice that comes from a sincere heart is good and obeying the Word of the Lord is better.

We see disobedience in the life of King Saul.

> Samuel said, Has the LORD as great a delight in burnt offerings and sacrifices as in obedience to the voice of the LORD? Behold, to obey is better than sacrifice, and to heed [is better] than the fat of rams. For rebellion is as [serious as] the sin of divination (fortune-telling), and disobedience is as [serious as] false

> religion and idolatry. Because you have rejected the word of the Lord, He also has rejected you as king. (1 Samuel 15:22-23 AMP)

The Lord takes great delight in our obedience. He is pleased when we do what He desires.

This scripture portion tells of King Saul not obeying the Word of the Lord given through the prophet Samuel. Saul could have obeyed God. This would have shown a love for God. Instead, he followed his own wishes and disobeyed God.

In John 14:15, our love for Jesus is shown in our following and living His commandments. A commandment is a directive that someone with authority gives. The priests under the Law had authority and Jesus has authority – they were both legitimate authorities because their authority comes from God.

Of course, these are not suggestions to consider but serious commandments from Almighty God. But Jesus does not give us God's commands without the ability to follow and do them.

> And I will ask the Father, and he will give you another Advocate, who will never leave you. He is the Holy Spirit, who leads into all truth. The world

> cannot receive him, because it isn't looking for him and doesn't recognize him. But you know him, because he lives with you now and later will be in you. No, I will not abandon you as orphans—I will come to you. (John 14:16-18 NLT)

Jesus told the disciples to wait in Jerusalem and receive the gift of the Holy Spirit that was promised by the Father. (Acts 1:4) The disciples would receive power from God through the giving of the Holy Spirit.

> But you will receive power when the Holy Spirit comes on you and you will be my witnesses in Jerusalem, and in all Judea and Samaria, and to the ends of the earth. (Acts 1:8 NIV)

God would enable them with His power. They could now go to the world and bring people Jesus Christ. The disciples were changed by God and would not be reluctant and timid. Now they would <u>want</u> to take Jesus' command and carry it out in the power of the Holy Spirit. Jesus commands us and the Holy Spirit brings the motivation and power of God. In all of this, believers obey and successfully do the works of God.

Today, believers are still called to obey and follow Jesus. The commands of God are still in effect and still valid for us. We "shall receive power" when the Holy Spirit comes on us and goes within us. Believers are equipped, given His authority and told to go. We are not orphans that have been abandoned but followers who are properly prepared to succeed for God.

When an employer tells an employee to complete a financial transaction for the company, it is the employer's responsibility to give them the needed finances. The boss provides for the worker's needs to complete the task. If the employer did not provide, they would not be an effective employer.

Our God is good and He always provides for His children. He has sent the Church into the world to bring change to the world and help people find, know and love God. His commission, His provision and His salvation. He calls, He provides and He saves people.

The Gospels tell us to follow Jesus. He has called people to come to Him and be His followers. Followers follow the lead of the Master. Disciples receive the teaching of the Teacher. I follow God and am His friend and servant because I love Him

The song *O How I Love Jesus* by Frederick Whitfield expresses the deep love that the believer has for Jesus.

There is a name I love to hear,

I love to sing its worth;

It sounds like music in my ear,

The sweetest name on earth.

O how I love Jesus,

O how I love Jesus,

O how I love Jesus,

Because He first loved me.

This traditional song clearly expresses why we follow and serve God.

We follow Him because of the deep love that each believer has for Jesus. We have a deep respect for Him. The love He has for His Body the Church is what motivates the believer to obey Him. I choose to obey Him because I love Him, not because I am a slave driven by a cruel master. I am a willing, loving servant of God who serves Him.

David was a young man who loved God. We know he was faithful and devoted in His duties as a shepherd. He had the same consistent faithfulness and devotion to God.

David understood the purposes of his life very clearly – love God and serve God. He understood God's protection and served Him until he died.

> I love you, LORD, my strength. (Psalm 18:1 NIV)

> Now when David had served God's purpose in his own generation, he fell asleep; he was buried with his ancestors and his body decayed. (Acts 13:36 NIV)

David understood that God loved Him and took care of Him. He understood the purposes that God had for him. He was quick to obey and quick to repent when he sinned and when he failed God.

> Let all that I am praise the LORD; with my whole heart, I will praise his holy name. Let all that I am praise the LORD; may I never forget the good things he does for me. He forgives all my sins and heals all my diseases. He redeems me from death and crowns me with love and tender mercies. He fills my life with good things. My youth is renewed like the eagle's! (Psalm 103:1-5 NLT)

> O my soul, bless GOD. From head to toe, I'll bless his holy name! O my soul, bless GOD, don't forget a single blessing! He forgives your sins - every one. He heals your diseases - every one. He redeems you from hell - saves your life! He crowns you with love and mercy - a paradise crown. He wraps you in goodness - beauty eternal. He renews your youth - you're always young in his presence. (Psalm 103:1-5 MSG)

David praised the Lord with his entire being. He was all-in for God. He wrote about Him, spoke about Him and danced before Him with great excitement!

The Bible says that David was a man after God's own heart. David knew God in a relationship of obedience, respect and friendship. On the other hand, King Saul disobeyed God and sinned. God took the Kingdom of Israel from him. God then sent the prophet Samuel to anoint David to be the new King of Israel.

> But now your kingdom will not endure; the LORD has sought out a man after his own heart and appointed him ruler of his people, because you have not kept the LORD's command. (1 Samuel 13:14 NIV)

> After removing Saul, he made David
> their king. God testified concerning him:
> 'I have found David son of Jesse, a man
> after my own heart; he will do everything
> I want him to do.' (Acts 13:22 NIV)

David followed God and learned what a relationship with God was really like, and what it was supposed to be.

> Hear, O Israel: The LORD our God,
> the LORD *is* one! You shall love
> the LORD your God with all your heart,
> with all your soul, and with all your
> strength. And these words which I
> command you today shall be in your
> heart. (Deuteronomy 6:4-6 NKJV)

> Listen, O Israel! The LORD is our God,
> the LORD alone. And you must love the
> LORD your God with all your heart, all
> your soul, and all your strength. And you
> must commit yourselves wholeheartedly
> to these commands that I am giving you
> today. (Deuteronomy 6:4-6 NLT)

I have always been interested in David. He understood a proper relationship with God. However, we know he sinned. He was an adulterer and a murderer. (2 Samuel 11)

> David did *what was* right in the eyes of
> the LORD, and had not turned aside from

> anything that He commanded him all the days of his life, except in the matter of Uriah the Hittite. (1 Kings 15:5 NKJV)

David pleased God because he did what was *right* – this word helps us know the he was righteous and upright. David knew he was nothing without God and that his success as a king and a man was dependent upon God's grace and mercy. David also knew that his sin was an act of disobedience and offensive to God.

David said that God had never abandoned His righteous children.

> I have been young, and now am old; yet have I not seen the righteous forsaken, nor his seed begging bread. (Psalm 37:25 KJV)

> I have been young and now I am old, yet I have not seen the righteous (those in right standing with God) abandoned or his descendants pleading for bread. (Psalm 37:25 AMP)

Today, God will not and does not abandon His people. His Word is His bond and He will keep us, not get rid of us! This is a truth that believers know and live.

We will be prepared and readied to serve Him as we keep His commandments and work together with God.

> So Christ himself gave the apostles, the prophets, the evangelists, the pastors and teachers, to equip his people for works of service, so that the body of Christ may be built up until we all reach unity in the faith and in the knowledge of the Son of God and become mature, attaining to the whole measure of the fullness of Christ. (Ephesians 4:11-13 NIV)

God gave people for leadership positions in the Body of Christ so that believers can help strengthen and train others in the Church. God expects the entire congregation to assist the leaders as they care for the people of God. Pastors are called as shepherds over the flock.

> Care for the flock that God has entrusted to you. Watch over it willingly, not grudgingly - not for what you will get out of it, but because you are eager to serve God. (1 Peter 5:2 NLT)

Everyone has a job in the Body of Christ. Leadership, workers, and all of those who contribute to the effort. Jesus gives everyone a job as a member of His Body.

Some are called to serve in the local congregation. Some are called to serve God by defending His honor before people.

The three Hebrew young men mentioned in Daniel obeyed God when they refused to worship Nebuchadnezzar's golden statue. They chose to serve God and <u>not</u> serve the idol.

> Shadrach, Meshach, and Abednego replied, "O Nebuchadnezzar, we do not need to defend ourselves before you. If we are thrown into the blazing furnace, the God whom we serve is able to save us. He will rescue us from your power, Your Majesty. But even if he doesn't, we want to make it clear to you, Your Majesty, that we will never serve your gods or worship the gold statue you have set up." (Daniel 3:16-18 NLT)

I believe that Shadrach, Meshach, and Abednego could have denied God and bowed down to the golden image. This would have brought about very different results. But they knew that personally obeying the commands of God was a critical part of their righteousness. A righteous person listens, hears and acts in obedience to God. As good Jewish young men, they would have clearly understood that bowing to idols was strictly forbidden.

> You shall have no other gods before me. You shall not make for yourself an image in the form of anything in heaven above or on the earth beneath or in the waters below. You shall not bow down to them or worship them; for I,
> the LORD your God, am a jealous God, (Exodus 20:3-5a NIV)

They knew that bowing to the idol was sin because it violated God's Law. In contrast, they knew that obeying God was a way to demonstrate our love for God. The Law and the Prophets teach this.

Jesus told us that we show our love for God by obeying Him. We fulfill the Law and the Prophets as we love and obey Him.

Believers obey God's commands because they love Him. The Church of Jesus Christ is here to do God's will.

> your kingdom come, your will be done, on earth as it is in heaven. (Matt 6.10 NIV)

God's love is clearly demonstrated in our obedience and our obedience clearly shows our love.

In closing, I believe the easy way to remember the necessity and advantage of obedience is found in the scriptures.

But Samuel replied, "What is more pleasing to the LORD: your burnt offerings and sacrifices or your obedience to his voice? Listen! Obedience is better than sacrifice, and submission is better than offering the fat of rams. (1 Samuel 15:22 AMP)

The response of every believer should be "Lord help to obey you with a sincere and truthful heart." As we follow God, let us also obey God. This is the sign of a genuine believer.

Obedience _is_ better than sacrifice.

Chapter Questions for Discussion or Study

1. How do we demonstrate our love for Jesus?

2. How did the disciples receive power from God?

3. Jesus told them that they would receive power. The disciples were to "go into all the world and _____."

4. What did David understand about his life with God?

5. King Saul and David both had different relationships with God. How were these relationships different?

6. FILL-IN: As we keep His commandments and work together with God, we will be _____ and _____ to serve Him.

7. Everyone has a job in the Body of Christ. What job are you responsible for?

8. Who were Shadrach, Meshach, and Abednego? What did they do to obey God?

9. How do believers today obey God like Shadrach, Meshach, and Abednego?

10. FILL-IN: Obedience is better than _____.

John 14

Chapter 8

I Am Going Away

Jesus made it very clear to His disciples. He would go away but that He would return.

> No, I will not abandon you as orphans - I will come to you. Soon the world will no longer see me, but you will see me. Since I live, you also will live. When I am raised to life again, you will know that I am in my Father, and you are in me, and I am in you. (John 14:18-20 NLT)

This news must have startled them. Sometimes it seems that the disciples were "thick-headed." For some reason, they just didn't understand. They were not like the religious leaders who had hard hearts. They were not ignorant - they had watched Jesus perform miracles and heard Him speak the entire time He ministered to people. I believe they were so overwhelmed by what Jesus told them that they were shocked. Today we would say "STOP! I'm in overload!" Jesus was leaving and they had never experienced anything like this – they knew He was God's Messiah, but now He was going. And on top of all this, Jesus was talking about His death and then coming back!

Why was all of this happening? Why was Jesus telling these things to the disciples? The scriptures clearly state that Jesus had to go through this – it was God's will for the Son of God.

> Surely he took up our pain and bore our suffering, yet we considered him punished by God, stricken by him, and afflicted. But he was pierced for our transgressions, he was crushed for our iniquities; the punishment that brought us peace was on him, and by his wounds we are healed. (Isaiah 53:4-5 NIV)

> He himself bore our sins in his body on the cross, so that we might die to sins and live for righteousness; by his wounds you have been healed. (1 Peter 2:24 NIV)

Jesus wanted the disciples to understand the "why" - why He was going to suffer and die, why He would go away and why He would return.

Without the brutal suffering and death Jesus experienced, the prophecies of His sacrifice could not be fulfilled. Because of the sacrifice of Jesus, the perfect and sinless Son of God, our sins were and are forgiven. Believers could now be born again and have a right relationship with God. Jesus actually took our sin, our burden and our separation from God upon Himself. He gave each of us His resurrection and brought us home to God.

All believers were made completely new because of His death, burial and resurrection. Healing, forgiveness and redemption were now guaranteed and could now become a reality for the people of the world.

> Therefore, if <u>anyone</u> is in Christ, the new creation has come: The old has gone, the new is here! (2 Corinthians 5:17 NIV, emphasis added)

We became brand new! The "old" previous things became dead and were buried. The new life replaced the old life. That is how we are brought back to God as new creatures. All of this is because Jesus died and was raised from the dead.

It is easy to take a scripture like 2 Corinthians 5:17 and considered to be religious jargon and then dismiss it. Jesus' resurrection actually happened and is in effect today. Believers have been made new creatures in Christ

Jesus. We can walk in this newness of life because of Him.

The entire history of the world pivots on Jesus' death on the cross and His resurrection from the dead. This is a BIG claim and may sound outrageous, but it's true. Jesus did more than some important religious thing. It was an act of love and our redemption from Jesus and the Father that was given to each of us – personally given to <u>you</u>.

Jesus told us that there are many mansions in His Father's house.

> In My Father's house are many mansions; if *it were* not *so,* I would have told you. I go to prepare a place for you. (John 14:2 NKJV)

> There is more than enough room in my Father's home. If this were not so, would I have told you that I am going to prepare a place for you? When everything is ready, I will come and get you, so that you will always be with me where I am. And you know the way to where I am going. (John 14:2-4 NLT)

It's clear that believers are invited to live in these mansions. The main idea here is Jesus wants us with Him for eternity.

People argue about what Jesus meant by *mansions*. The Greek word means dwelling place or where one can abide. It is used to show the indwelling of the Holy Spirit, His permanent residence within the believer. This word shows permanence, not a momentary stop. The scriptures are unclear whether the *mansion* looks like a Beverly Hills estate, a simple room or a "humble abode." Whatever it is, I will be with Jesus and that's the importance and reality of this. God will meet all of my needs in agreement with His riches (Greek – abundance of wealth or possessions) in glory. I will be happy and He will continually care for me - all of this shows God's love for His people.

The main issue for the disciples that night is "where is Jesus going?" (v.5) Jesus made it clear that He was going to the Father. He said He wouldn't have told the disciples this if He had not prepared a place for them. His resurrection would bring them and all believers home to the Father. This includes us and all future believers – we will have a home.

The next verse we see is John 14:6. Thomas (the disciple) exclaimed (v.5) that they could not figure out where Jesus was going.

> Jesus told him, I am the way, the truth, and the life. No one can come to the

Father except through me. (John 14:6 NLT)

Jesus made it clear that he was going to the Father and that people could only get to God through Jesus. Religion, philosophy, excellent moral behavior, giving away your money, etc. cannot get you to God. These things do not work. Jesus was tortured and crucified until dead for our sin, our sickness and our well-being in this life. When this was accomplished, God raised Him from the dead. This is the reason that we have eternal life.

The disciples asked Him why He would only reveal Himself to the disciples (v.21b) after He told them, "And I will love them and reveal myself to each of them." That question is still relevant today. People might ask you, "Why is God so real to you?" or comment to you, "You sure are religious."

The answer to these remarks is a simple one "because I know Jesus Christ and have a relationship with Him. You can know Him too." Christians are not some group or class of special-privileged people who think they are better than others. It all comes down to having a relationship with God through Jesus Christ. It's not earned with religious behavior or doing nice things for people. It's simply a matter of receiving salvation through Jesus. You must believe deep inside of you that Jesus was raised from the dead and that Jesus Christ is the Lord of your life. This is the simple prayer that brings you to God through Jesus Christ. It's not magic or good luck, it's sincere belief in the effective work of Jesus Christ.

But why would Jesus reveal Himself only to His followers? All believers in Jesus have a relationship with Him. They know Him and He knows them. Think about it – we tell our friends and family certain things that we might not tell someone else. I believe this is what Jesus was saying. People talk to God from their hearts and tell Him how things really are. This is the nature of a relationship – we talk, we listen, and we act. Believers imitate God – He talks, He listens and He acts on our behalf. This is the God of love who profoundly loves His people.

God will reveal Himself to <u>anyone</u> who searches for God in faith, listens to God and acts upon what He says. Abraham is an excellent example of someone who went to God in faith. God revealed Himself to Abraham because he had faith that God was real. Because of this faith, God spoke to Him and counted this faith as righteousness. Abraham was convinced that God was real and wanted a relationship with him.

> But without faith *it is* impossible to please *Him,* for he who comes to God must believe that He is, and *that* He is a rewarder of those who diligently seek Him. (Hebrews 11:6 NKJV)

> But without faith it is impossible to [walk with God and] please Him, for whoever comes [near] to God must [necessarily] believe that God exists and that He rewards those who [earnestly and diligently] seek Him. (Hebrews 11:6 AMP)

An unbeliever is someone who does not believe in God. Unbelievers are not just non-believers, their unbelief is the opposite of faith. A believer has faith and trusts in the goodness of God. They know that God is love and He purposely sent Jesus to redeem the world. The life of an unbeliever can be seen as the opposite of the life of Abraham who had a life of faith in God.

Unbelievers are not involved with God. Many unbelievers believe that there is no God because there is no physical evidence to confirm His existence. Some do not see their need to believe in God and see the best course of action is to rule their own lives with a human-centered philosophy.

If they do believe in the existence of God, many reckon Him as a hard taskmaster who is trying to punish people and deny them fun in their life! Others see Him as some old guy who has lost interest in people and really does not care anymore. To be a Christian, a person must believe that God is real and that He is alive. God cares deeply for the lives of people.

Many unbelievers see God as irrelevant. Their skepticism of His relevance governs their unbelief. These unbelievers would say, "God is a fable, a sign of mental instability and the silly beliefs of confused religious people. Why should I believe in God?"

Unbelievers are deceived by the devil and their own attitude of stubborn ignorance. Oddly, many unbelievers do not believe in the devil who is misleading them. The unbeliever embraces the evil trickery of the devil and justifies their reasoned thinking and the humanistic belief in the natural goodness of people. All of this is instead of believing in God.

The Bible states that everyone has sinned (Romans 3:23) and nobody is righteous in themselves. Despite all the morally admirable things that unbelieving people engage in, it does not forgive <u>their</u> sins.

Jesus came to earth to demonstrate a relationship with God and a sinless life of faith.

He was the perfect example of what faith and belief as well as living for God were really like. His life and faith were an inspiration that resulted in hope and is available for all humanity to accept and receive. Unbelief is truly a personal tragedy because it denies the salvation and love of God that Jesus has brought to everyone and God's infinite love for mankind.

The disciples were faced with the constant harassment of Jesus by the religious leaders. Jesus responded by teaching the people to have faith in God (Mark 11:22) and signs and wonders to help people.

> Now when He was in Jerusalem at the Passover feast, many believed in His name [identifying themselves with Him] after seeing His signs (attesting miracles) which He was doing. (John 2:23 AMP)

> A large crowd was following Him because they had seen the signs (attesting miracles) which He continually performed on those who were sick. (John 6:2 AMP)

Despite the constant harassment, the disciples made a sincere decision to follow Jesus. Peter even expressed, "You are the Messiah, the Son of the living God." (Matthew 16:16 NIV)

This expression of faith sharply contrasts with the vicious attacks of the religious leaders.

When Jesus taught or healed someone, the religious leaders objected to Him based on their manmade religious beliefs. Their negative reactions mischaracterized God. They distorted the scriptures and argued with Jesus to suit their unbelief. Even though Jesus was the Messiah and Son of God, they continued to criticize and object.

> When the Pharisees heard that Jesus had arrived, they came and immediately started to argue with him. Testing him, they demanded that he show them a miraculous sign from heaven to prove his authority. (Mark 8:11 NLT)
>
> And they were looking for a way to seize Him, but they were afraid of the crowd; for they knew that He spoke this parable in reference to [and as a charge against] them. And so they left Him and went away. Then they sent some of the Pharisees and Herodians to Jesus in order to trap Him into making a statement [that they could use against Him]. (Mark 12:12-13 AMP)
>
> "Woe to you, teachers of the law and Pharisees, you hypocrites! You build tombs for the prophets and decorate the

> graves of the righteous. And you say, 'If we had lived in the days of our ancestors, we would not have taken part with them in shedding the blood of the prophets.' (Matthew 23:29-30 NIV)

The rejection of Jesus by the unbelieving religious leaders was because of their hard heart.

> He was despised and rejected - a man of sorrows, acquainted with deepest grief. We turned our backs on him and looked the other way. He was despised, and we did not care. (Isaiah 53:3 NLT)

Jesus came to bring God's love and He was hated and forsaken. The religious unbelievers in the Gospels had met their match. As they hurled insults, He responded with the Word of God. Unbelievers need Jesus too!

In our present society, unbelievers are alive and well, and they still reject God. Unbelievers reject God by ignoring Him, denying His love and power and ridiculing believers. These are the same tactics that are reported in Acts. Whether it occurred during Bible times or in the here and now, it is unbelief and rejecting God.

God brings a day of decision to every person. It is the choice of every person to have belief or unbelief. Joshua addressed the people of

Israel and gave them a choice, they could believe in God and follow His ways or they could serve false gods. Belief or unbelief.

Jairus decided to believe. His daughter was dying and his family needed a miracle of healing from Jesus. There was a delay in Jesus arriving and his daughter died. They told Jesus He no longer had to go to his home. His daughter was dead.

> But when Jesus heard what had happened, he said to Jairus, "Don't be afraid. Just have faith, and she will be healed." When they arrived at the house, Jesus wouldn't let anyone go in with him except Peter, John, James, and the little girl's father and mother. The house was filled with people weeping and wailing, but he said, "Stop the weeping! She isn't dead; she's only asleep." But the crowd laughed at him because they all knew she had died. Then Jesus took her by the hand and said in a loud voice, "My child, get up!" And at that moment her life returned, and she immediately stood up! Then Jesus told them to give her something to eat. Her parents were overwhelmed, but Jesus insisted that they not tell anyone what had happened. (Luke 8:50-56 NLT)

Jairus chose to believe what Jesus was saying and reject unbelief. Jesus told Jairus, "Don't be afraid. Just have faith, and she will be healed." It has been said that if Jairus has stopped Jesus in unbelief and told Him "don't go to my house" his daughter would still be dead. Jairus' made a choice to believe – it was an act of faith in God. He heard Jesus, believed Jesus and followed Jesus.

Believers choose to trust their lives and their future to God. Jairus, the disciples, other people in the Bible and people throughout history have trusted and believed God. This is essential to a relationship with God through Jesus Christ.

John 14 describes the night before the crucifixion. At this time, Jesus explained many things to His disciples – something that would help them go forward after He left. They would go to bring the Gospel to everyone, heal the sick and raise the dead.

Jesus was preparing His disciples for the future. He would send the Holy Spirit who would protect and keep the Church, the Body of Christ. We also follow Christ and receive the presence of God. Believers are in fellowship with God the Holy Spirit and kept by the sure protection of God.

Today, Jesus is not on the earth. God has sent the Holy Spirit. "But the Advocate, the Holy Spirit, whom the Father will send in my name, will teach you all things and will remind you of everything I have said to you." (John 14:26 NIV)

Believers can be confident and sure that in spite of Jesus going away, He will come again. The Holy Spirit is here and ready to help us as we work together with Him. Thank God.

Chapter Questions for Discussion or Study

1. Jesus made it very clear to His disciples. He would _____ but that He would _____.

2. Why were the disciples shocked when Jesus told them He was going away?

3. Why did Jesus have to suffer and die?

4. FILL-IN: 1 Peter 2:24 NIV - He himself bore our sins in his body on the cross, so that we might die to sins and live for righteousness;

   _____.

5. 1 Corinthians 5:15 – What happens when anyone is in Christ?

6. How does God bless the believer who is in Christ?

7. What does the word *mansions* tell believers? What are God's intentions?

8. Describe what believers and unbelievers accept as being "true" about God?

9. How are believers different from unbelievers?

10. FILL-IN: Hebrews 11:6 NKJV - But without _____ *it is* impossible to please *Him,* for he who comes to God must _____ that He is, and *that* He is a rewarder of those who _____ seek Him.

11. Why were the religious leaders opposed to Jesus? Why do people oppose Jesus today?

John 15
Chapter 9
The Peace of God

God's peace is one of the greatest gifts that He gives us. We cannot earn it, buy it or manufacture it. It is a gift – pure and simple. God gives us His peace.

> Peace I leave with you, My peace I give to you; not as the world gives do I give to you. Let not your heart be troubled, neither let it be afraid. (John 14:27 NKJV)

> I am leaving you with a gift—peace of mind and heart. And the peace I give is a gift the world cannot give. So don't be troubled or afraid. (John 14:27 NLT)

The world is a wild place and it is a big mess. The world is filled with confusion and pressure. Society shows the effects of these conditions in wars, political chaos and instability in people's lives. In times past the stresses of life were probably as bad or worse than today. The big difference today is the 24-hour, computer-driven, online society we have become. The love of money and possessions have become the new norm. As an example, American opinion and trends are driven by online social media. A person, movement or government can win or lose the public opinion struggle based solely on online reactions. With 24-hour television, trends begin and end in a few hours. America is now so prosperous that a reasonable income is considered insufficient because it does not guarantee a luxurious lifestyle.

The only answer is God's peace. This peace is exclusively available through life in Jesus Christ.

> And the peace of God, which transcends all understanding, will guard your hearts and your minds in Christ Jesus. (Philippians 4:7 NIV)

Peace is often defined as an absence of war or conflict within society, tranquility and freedom from disturbance. After World War II, Europe experienced a short-lived period of peace before the Cold War escalated into an international problem that disrupted lives and countries.

The peace of God is different because it is within the soul of man. The Greek word for peace describes the tranquil state of a soul assured of its salvation through Christ. The individual has a relationship with God and is content with His provision in our lives. The peace of God offers a new and better alternative to the pressures of this world. Instead of being "driven and agitated," God's peace brings calmness as the believer trusts and believes God.

The scripture in Philippians tells us that His peace "transcends all understanding." This peace goes beyond human comprehension in the believer's life. God's peace changes the struggle and striving life and replaces it with God's peace, trust in Him and a life of faith. Christianity is unique because it brings peace from God.

This peace amazes people and challenges them with this question – "how can following God make a person peaceful?" Christ alone brought this peace to the believer by reconciling us personally to God.

> For God was pleased to have all his fullness dwell in him, and through him to reconcile to himself all things, whether things on earth or things in heaven, by making peace through his blood, shed on the cross. (Colossians 1:19-20 NIV)

Jesus made peace for us with God. He broke down the barrier created by sin and brought us home to God. It is beautiful to know that God loves you, He is not angry with you and wants you to choose to come home to Him.

The peace that believers experience and live in Christ is based upon the Hebrew word *shalom*. It means safe, well, happy, friendly, health and prosperity. God's wonderful peace is meant to abide in a person permanently. People often greet and say farewell with *"shalom."* When they do this, they are giving them these wonderful blessings.

The root meaning of the Hebrew word *shalom* are found in the English word *peace*.

> I will both lie down in peace, and sleep; for You alone, O LORD, make me dwell in safety. (Psalm 4:8 NKJV)

This verse shows a person who can trust God with their life and relax in God without being driven by issues and controversies that rob them of their peace.

> In His days the righteous shall flourish, and abundance of peace, until the moon is no more. (Psalm 72:7 NKJV)

The righteous have a relationship with God that brings about His shalom (peace) in our lives.

> I listen carefully to what God the LORD is saying, for he speaks peace to his

> faithful people. But let them not return to their foolish ways. (Psalm 85:8 NLT)

We listen to and follow God. We learn His ways and make them how we live. We turn away from making bad choices and change by making "God choices" as a way of life.

Believers become carriers of His peace and we distribute it to the world.

> How beautiful on the mountains are the feet of the messenger who brings good news, the good news of peace and salvation, the news that the God of Israel reigns! (Isaiah 52:7 NLT)

Beautiful feet show that carrying the gospel pleases God and brings a pleasant and eternal gift offered to everyone – the love of God. Salvation from God through Jesus Christ brings the true and unshakeable reality of God's peace.

> And Gideon built an altar to the LORD there and named it Yahweh-Shalom (which means "the LORD is peace"). (Judges 24:24 NLT)

God called Gideon to rescue Israel from Midian. Gideon would have to confront a formidable enemy. The challenge was overcome by God when the Spirit of God clothed Gideon with power. I believe this is where God's peace made him "God confident" and he began to truly trust God. Gideon understood that his own ability was insufficient to rescue Israel, but with God, he was fully equipped. God makes all things are possible!

This peace allowed Gideon to rescue God's people so they could live their lives in peace.

Peace is a precious commodity that people desperately seek. "I wish I could have peace of mind" or "there is no peace in my family – how can we find peace?" Some people have grown so calloused without peace and conditioned themselves to endure the daily controversies we encounter. But inner, permanent peace is far beyond what humans are capable of understanding. God's peace transcends human reason.

Jesus walked daily in the peace of God and readily carried it to the people. Jesus endured great suffering on the cross. Besides the extreme physical beating, He took all of the sin of mankind upon Himself, gave up His close fellowship with the Father and bought mankind's freedom from sin. Jesus was the perfect sacrifice of God for each of us - the Lamb of God who takes away the sin of the world! (John 1:29 NLT) This is still true for us today.

How could Jesus willingly go to the cross and experience the abuse, the suffering and the pain? How could one man endure this extreme abuse knowing he would soon be crucified?

In Matthew 26, we read that Jesus resolved to obey God. Jesus was fully committed to the mission – save and restore people to God.

> He went a little farther and fell on His face, and prayed, saying, "O My Father, if it is possible, let this cup pass from Me; nevertheless, not as I will, but as You *will.*" (Matthew 26:39 NLT)

Jesus was fully aware that He would suffer and die. For this reason, He expressed the same human emotion as we do. He asked God if there was another way to bring redemption to people. With unshakeable faith and extreme trust in God, Jesus told the Father "not as I will, but as You will." Jesus told God that He would go through with it because it is what the Father had planned. It was Jesus' responsibility to be God's perfect, sinless sacrifice and die for all the sin of mankind on the cross. This was not just a normal Roman execution. It was the Father sacrificing His Son and fulfilling His plan to bring redemption for all who would receive it.

After the resurrection, Jesus came to the disciples and told them that He was sending them to serve God. They would preach the Gospel, heal the sick and raise the dead.

> "Peace be with you! As the Father has sent me, I am sending you." And with that he breathed on them and said, "Receive the Holy Spirit. (John 20:21-22 NIV)

Jesus blessed them with peace and with the Holy Spirit. He was giving them God's peace and power and then sending them on their mission – "take the Gospel to the world."

> And Jesus came and spoke to them, saying, "All authority has been given to Me in heaven and on earth. Go therefore and make disciples of all the nations, baptizing them in the name of the Father and of the Son and of the Holy Spirit, teaching them to observe all things that I have commanded you; and lo, I am with you always, *even* to the end of the age." Amen. (Matthew 28:18-20 KJV)

The disciples were *sent* and we are *sent*. Christ inserted the disciples and us into situations, some of which were really difficult. But we were given the peace of God that Jesus had received from the Father. "MY peace I GIVE you." (Emphasis added) Jesus had peace to serve God, to be burdened with our sin and endure a cruel crucifixion that ended with His death, burial and glorious resurrection.

> But He was wounded for our transgressions, He was crushed for our wickedness [our sin, our injustice, our wrongdoing]; the punishment [required] for our well-being *fell* on Him, and by His stripes (wounds) we are healed. (Isaiah 53:5 AMP)

He could face His suffering and death with courage and faith because He lived a life that was strong in God's peace. Believers can confidently trust God as they go through challenges, persecutions and problems. God protected Jesus and God will protect us. We see this loving protection in the Holy Scriptures.

> Even though I walk through the [sunless] valley of the shadow of death, I fear no evil, for You are with me; Your rod [to protect] and Your staff [to guide], they comfort *and* console me. (Psalm 23:4 AMP)

> For thou wilt not leave my soul in hell; neither wilt thou suffer thine Holy One to see corruption. (Psalm 16:10 KJV)

Whatever God sends each of us to do, He will always keep us. When He calls and sends, He provides and protects.

We engage with God through faith and He sends the Holy Spirit to give us the power to do what He wants. God's peace causes us to endure and prevail through difficult times. God's peace keeps us trusting Him and staying in communication with Him.

Noah walked in peace with God. By definition, we saw that peace (shalom) is safety, wellness, happiness, friendship, health and prosperity. Noah had a relationship with God and enjoyed a life of God's peace.

God called Noah to build a HUGE boat. (Genesis 6) This was before we had Lowe's and Home Depot to purchase building supplies. Noah would have to obtain all of the planks to build the boat. God's peace would have been a necessity to complete this project. Make no mistake, the work was exhausting and difficult. But remember, Noah had a BIG God who helps him.

Noah was alive years before Proverbs was written. Proverbs clearly describes what Noah had to do to stay at peace while undertaking and accomplishing something that is near impossible in human terms.

Trust in the LORD with all your heart and lean not on your own understanding; in all your ways submit to him, and he will make your paths straight. (Proverbs 3:5-6 NIV)

Trust GOD from the bottom of your heart; don't try to figure out everything on your own. Listen for GOD's voice in everything you do, everywhere you go; he's the one who will keep you on track. (Proverbs 3:5-6 MSG)

- Noah completely trusted God more than he trusted anyone or anything.
- Noah did not use <u>his</u> thinking in this venture, he received direction from God.
- Noah "bowed the knee" to God in everything – obedience at any cost.

God made His paths straight – He showed Noah where to go and who to deal with. It's like God taking all of the curves and bumps out of the road to allow a person to travel safely and have a good trip. The KJV tells us that "He shall direct thy paths." God's goodness is shown with our Father keeping us clearly directed and following the best path.

The peace we have in Christ through faith is explained clearly through this Proverb – totally trust God, rely on God for direction and always obey Him. This is how Jesus lived His life with His Father. This is how we live our lives with God. In this we experience His peace.

God wants us to make and carry this peace to others.

> Follow peace with all men, and holiness, without which no man shall see the Lord (Hebrews 12:14 KJV)

> Work at living in peace with everyone, and work at living a holy life, for those who are not holy will not see the Lord. (Hebrews 12:14 NLT)

Believers work to live a life of peace in our relationships with others. It should be the believer that brings God's peace into tough situations.

How does a believer bring peace and live peace? The "how-to" comes through the leading and power of the Holy Spirit. He will direct your paths and get you in place to make a difference. We are the representatives and ambassadors for Christ. Our mission is to bring God's peace to people. Carrying God's peace is another way to serve our God and King.

In the blessings found in Numbers 6:24-26, God tells Moses that He will bless the people.

The LORD bless you and keep you;
The LORD make His face shine upon you, And be gracious to you;
The LORD lift up His countenance upon you, And give you peace. (Numbers 6:24-26 NKJV)

May the LORD bless you and protect you. May the LORD smile on you and be gracious to you. May the LORD show you his favor and give you his peace. (Numbers 6:24-26 NLT)

GOD bless you and keep you, GOD smile on you and gift you, GOD look you full in the face and make you prosper. (Numbers 6:24-26 MSG)

The priests are to tell the people that God will bless them, protect them, smile upon them, and show them His favor. In addition, He will give the people His *shalom*, His peace. This is important because we walk through life and face all of life's pressures on a day-to-day basis, just as Noah did. We might not be building a boat, but the pressure is still a factor. God is constantly blessing us in all areas of our life. In this, we receive His peace. With His peace, we can endure and successfully triumph over our problems and challenges.

In closing, God's peace is so much greater, infinitely greater than anything that people can even begin to comprehend. God's peace is simple for people – receive Christ as Lord, walk in a relationship of trusting Him and live your life for God. Believers live a life of the peace of God because of Christ. We must always be sure to choose to follow God and allow His peace to prevail.

Thank God for His peace. Lord, help us to always walk in Your peace.

Chapter Questions for Discussion or Study

1. Why is the peace of God one of the most important gifts that God gives to believers?

2. How do believers get the peace of God?

3. Why is God's peace different and better than what people define as "peace?"

4. FILL-IN: The righteous have a _____ with God that brings about His _____ (peace) in our lives.

5. God called Gideon to defeat Midian. God brought peace to Gideon so he could obey God. Why was this important?

6. Describe a time when Jesus had to live in God's peace to accomplish God's will?

7. FILL-IN: He (Jesus) could face His suffering and death with _____ because He lived a life that was strong in God's _____.

8. Believers should trust God, rely on Him for direction, and always obey Him. Why is this important?

John 14
Chapter 10
God Puts A Dream In Your Heart

God puts His dreams and a knowledge of His will inside each of us. These dreams inspire and motivate us. Some of these dreams are planted at an early age. Kids often say, "When I grow up, I want to be..." Other plans come to us as we mature and start to gain an understanding of life.

John Wooden was a highly successful basketball coach at UCLA several years ago. He won the NCAA Tournament many times and was a motivational influence on his team. He said

> *Don't give up on your dreams, or your dreams will give up on you.* - John Wooden

This quote inspires me to <u>actively</u> pursue the dreams God gives me, which I accept and make my dreams. It takes more than talking and thinking about dreams. It takes action and tenacity to pursue our dream. Some dreams happen quickly and some take a lifetime to obtain and this is why action and tenacity are critical. When we persevere in pursuing our dreams, we will receive them.

But God is different than people. Besides giving us dreams and aspirations, He is constant and He never quits on us.

> I am with you always [remaining with you perpetually—regardless of circumstance, and on every occasion], even to the end of the age. (Matthew 28:20 AMP)

We delight in Him. We love Him, and hold Him as the GREATEST thing in our lives. He plants His desires in our hearts and minds and enables us to follow them.

> Delight yourself in the LORD, And He will give you the desires *and* petitions of your heart. (Psalm 37:4 AMP)

We have the dreams which God gives us. The goals will come from God as we actively pursue our relationship with Him.

He gave us things to do in the form of commands and invitations. He said He will always be with us. He <u>never</u> said, "I will abandon you when you make a mistake or fail." We pursue the dreams that come from Him, following Him in the power of the Holy Spirit. If we fail, we start over and do it again.

I have and follow my dreams that come from God. I was swimming in the Rappahannock River with my dog one hot summer day back in the late 1970s. It was funny because I was swimming around and suddenly realized that the Lord was speaking to me. I could not hear Him with my ears, but I could sense His still small voice down inside of me. I never expected it that day but was thrilled to receive it from God.

God spoke to me that day from the scriptures in Isaiah 61.

> The Spirit of the Sovereign LORD is on me, because the LORD has anointed me to proclaim good news to the poor. (Isaiah 61:1 NIV)

I suddenly realized that this scripture was revealed to me from the Lord. He told me "you are called to preach and teach the Gospel." I was so excited and motivated to go that day and start preaching to anyone and everyone! I remember thinking that summer that I would start a ministry and travel the world. I wanted this to all happen NOW! These were my ideas and plans but they were not God's ideas and plans. He called me to preach, but I "grew" His desires for me into something else that I had conceived and wanted. I believe my heart was right, but I was adding to God's will. He called me and I added to the dream.

We should actively pursue our dreams from God, but more than the dreams, we should seek God. By that I mean that we should make loving God, following God, obeying God and listening to God more important than what we <u>do</u> for God.

In addition to this, I just wasn't ready. I felt ready, but God needed to prepare and train me. I could have done this or that, but I wasn't prepared and ready. I was on MY time, not God's time.

This is where I want to interject that following <u>our</u> own self-made dreams can get us into trouble. What I finally realized later was that God had plans and dreams for me. I was responsible for finding, learning and knowing His will for me. What did God want? What was His time? What do I need to do today? These questions are answered through the Word of God – reading and meditating on it, talking and listening to God in prayer and being involved with the family of God in a local Bible-based church.

How did I find the will of God? First, let me say it was a progressive 40 year-long process. Sometimes, I gave up and later repented to return to His program. It took a lot of learning of the Word of God and putting it into practice. It involved failing and starting over in the process and refusing to quit! God worked with me, and my pastors worked with me. My Christian friends and family worked with me. And guess what? I finally learned His will for me. It was a long process but well worth the time and effort.

While going through the process, I kept asking God – "when Lord? When are You going to do something?" I knew I was growing, but I wanted it <u>now</u>! It was typical modern American thinking. We want instant this and instant that. God's ways are not our ways. God's ways are greater and perfect.

We must receive our dreams from God and not follow other pursuits. I am a school teacher by training and had a personal dream to be a school administrator. The desire was intense - I wanted it really bad. It was better money and, very honestly, carried more prestige. But I also knew that it was not God's will. I was called to preach and teach the Gospel of Jesus Christ.

Finally, I took a job as a high school assistant principal. I was excited! I could now put all of my knowledge and experiences into practice. I took the job but was let go without cause before my 90-day review. During the dismissal meeting, I could hear in my heart, "all things work together for good for those who love God and are called according to His purpose." (Romans 8:28) even though I was being let go, I knew God was on the scene! I was at peace knowing God understood and acted on my behalf.

> The LORD is for me, so I will have no fear. What can mere people do to me? (Psalm 118:6 NLT)

It was somewhat funny. I was getting sacked and it didn't faze me – God was working and I would be OK! I was now entering a new phase in my life. Another adventure with Jesus! I didn't know what to do except trust God and wait for Him.

As the believer waits on the Lord, they actively worship Him, knowing that He will act.

> Wait patiently for the LORD. Be brave and courageous. Yes, wait patiently for the LORD. (Psalm 27:14 NLT)

> The Lord is not slow in keeping his promise, as some understand slowness. Instead he is patient with you, not wanting anyone to perish, but everyone to come to repentance. But the day of the Lord will come like a thief. (2 Peter 3:9-10a NIV)

The word *wait* in Psalm 27 means to look eagerly for, to hope and expect, to linger for something or to lie in wait. When we *wait* on the Lord, we know deep inside that He will move and act in our best interest. We are confident and convinced!

So waiting on the Lord tells us that God will act according to His wishes based on His timing. His timing is the right timing. He calls us and we follow Him. When we use self-determination based on our schedule, we usually get it wrong. God is all-knowing (omniscient); when we deal with Him, He tells us the right time to go or stop and the right place to go or not. He reveals things to us and helps us succeed. He is a good God who loves His children.

I have learned to be confident and expectant, knowing God will work in my best interests. Sometimes it is a "yes" from God, sometimes a "wait" or a "no." Maybe you hear "go here" or "go there," "talk to that person," or "pray for that guy."

If we will wait on the Lord and follow His direction, we will succeed in following God's directions and do it in God's timing.

> But they that wait upon the LORD shall renew their strength; they shall mount up with wings as eagles; they shall run,

> and not be weary; and they shall walk, and not faint. (Isaiah 40:31 KJV)

> But those who wait for the LORD [who expect, look for, and hope in Him] Will gain new strength *and* renew their power; They will lift up their wings [and rise up close to God] like eagles [rising toward the sun]; They will run and not become weary, They will walk and not grow tired. (Isaiah 40:31 AMP)

God will give us His strength to endure and be successful. Along with this strength comes a confident expectation – "God will help me!"

We can see this waiting on God in the life of Abram (later Abraham).

> The LORD had said to Abram, "Go from your country, your people and your father's household to the land I will show you. (Genesis 12:1 NIV)

> So Abram went, as the LORD had told him; and Lot went with him. Abram was seventy-five years old when he set out from Harran. (Genesis 12: 4 NIV)

Abram heard the voice of God, packed up and left his home in Harran. He followed God's leading "to the land I will show you." Abram was faithful to listen and do what God said. He waited confidently on God and was blessed to receive the promise from God.

Abraham walked in the dreams that God gave to Him.

Today, believers walk in the dreams that God sends. Believers will receive His guidance as they trust in Him.

> Trust in *and* rely confidently on the LORD with all your heart And do not rely on your own
> insight *or* understanding. In all your ways know and acknowledge *and* recognize Him, And He will make your paths straight *and* smooth [removing obstacles that block your way]. (Proverbs 3:5-6 AMP)

> Trust in the LORD with all your heart; do not depend on your own understanding. Seek his will in all you do, and he will show you which path to take. (Proverbs 3:5-6 NLT)

This is what Abraham did. He actively trusted God and in doing this, he obeyed God. I am sure that Abraham had dreams of having a child. God fulfilled that dream with the birth of Isaac.

What is your dream? Today is the day to confidently believe in God for His dream for you and then trust Him to bring it to pass. As one man said "don't put God on the clock," meaning that we must rely on, trust and follow His wishes and His timetable for us.

Trust God today. Know God and live the dreams that come from Him. God will bless you.

Chapter Questions for Discussion or Study

1. What does the quote from Coach John Wooden mean to you?

2. Why should we pursue the dreams that God has for each of us?

3. What will God do when you delight yourself in the Lord? (see Psalm 37:4)

4. Describe a time when God revealed His dreams for you

5. Why should believers pursue God more than pursuing His dreams for them?

6. Why should a believer <u>always</u> be ready to hear from God?

7. What does Romans 8:28 mean in the life of a believer? What does this scripture mean in your life?

8. What does the word *wait* mean?

9. FILL-IN: Isaiah 40:31 KJV - But they that _____ upon the LORD shall renew their strength; they shall mount up with _____; they shall _____, and not be weary; and they shall _____, and not faint.

10. Why should a believer do things on God's timing?

11. Why is it important not to put God "on the clock?" Describe things you have done to find and follow God's dreams and timing.

12. What did Abraham do to demonstrate his trust in God?

John 15
Preface

In the 15th chapter, John speaks clearly about the future relationship between Jesus and His church. He does this through an examination of a grapevine and the attached branches. This parable is a GREAT way to understand how Jesus Christ and His church interact. Believers can begin to comprehend the nature and characteristics of life in Christ, which involves a lot of "give and take" with God.

Believers will see the permanent nature of this life in the True Vine. It is not temporary or transient but meant to be an active give and take with God that will last for eternity.

Persecution and hatred for the believer are everyday aspects of the Christian life. Jesus was hated because He told people that God loved them and that they should give up their life to embrace life for God. The world hates believers for the same reasons.

I hope you enjoy John 15 and what I have written in these chapters.

Be blessed!

John 15
Chapter 1
The Real Thing

Jesus said that He is the True Vine.

> I am the true vine, and my Father is the husbandman. (John 15:1 KJV)

> I am the true grapevine, and my Father is the gardener. (John 15:1 NLT)

Jesus, the True Vine, is genuine. He is the legitimate vine and not some imitation plastic vine. The world offers us the imitation and Jesus tells us that He is genuine. After He likens Himself to a vine, He tells us that the Father is the gardener – the caretaker and owner of the vineyard.

In nature, vines and branches have a life-giving and life-sustaining relationship. Every tended vine has someone responsible for it. When you see a beautiful vineyard, please know that someone cares for it.

The Greek word for *true* means the <u>opposite</u> of fiction, counterfeit, imaginary or pretend. Something true can be relied upon. These words tell us that the True Vine can be trusted

– He is exactly what He says. Jesus, the True Vine is our Lord and a genuine friend, someone who does not misrepresent Himself and is not a fraud. A relationship with Him is *true*, genuine and can be trusted.

People join themselves to all sorts of "vines" that are not legitimate – "vines" like money, sex, possessions, power, etc. These "vines" are meant to be replacements for God.

The U.S. has about $70 million of counterfeit money in circulation that is not legitimate U.S. currency. The bills might look good, but they are as false as a liar who doesn't tell the truth.

Some people claim that there are many "ways to God." They are all counterfeit and none of these ways to God are legitimate - they just don't work. Receiving Jesus as Lord and Savior and establishing a relationship with Him is the only way to God and the only means to get a fulfilled life.

The word I like most about Jesus is *perfect*. Our Lord and Savior, Jesus Christ is perfect. He has no flaws or shortcomings and He is never confused or without an answer. Jesus does not have to guess and hope He is right.

Unbelievers do not understand that God is perfect – perfect love, perfect character and a perfect plan for your life. We see this in the words of the prophet Jeremiah.

> For I know the thoughts that I think toward you, saith the LORD, thoughts of peace, and not of evil, to give you an expected end. Then shall ye call upon me, and ye shall go and pray unto me, and I will hearken unto you. And ye shall seek me, and find me, when ye shall search for me with all your heart. (Jeremiah 29:11-13 KJV)

> I know what I'm doing. I have it all planned out—plans to take care of you, not abandon you, plans to give you the future you hope for. "When you call on me, when you come and pray to me, I'll listen. "When you come looking for me, you'll find me. "Yes, when you get serious about finding me and want it more than anything else, I'll make sure you won't be disappointed." (Jeremiah 29:10-13 MSG)

The context of this verse is God's children being bound in captivity. This is the case when we are attached to an illegitimate vine, a type of captivity – we are hooked up to a false source. This is a counterfeit way of life that acts as if it is good and satisfying when actually it is death. The True Vine keeps us spiritually healthy when we are attached to Him.

God thinks about us continually. He brings us peace and gives us an expected end that He has planned out. As we abide in Him, His plans for us come to pass because He is in charge. When we totally trust Him, when He is totally important to us, we will find Him. When we are totally committed to being connected with Him, we will be abiding in the vine, Jesus the True Vine.

Jesus, the True Vine has a plan for your life. The plan is real, genuine and legitimate. The devil is the illegitimate vine that wants destruction for you.

> The thief's purpose is to steal and kill and destroy. My purpose is to give them a rich and satisfying life. (John 10:10 NLT)

The devil and his followers who do his bidding are only out to hurt you. They are deceptive, cruel, full of hate and totally anti-God. He tells people that he is a big shot who is equal to God. In reality, the devil is nothing more than a rebellious, fallen angel who hates God. The devil's followers are deceived and live their lives doing evil. They steal, kill and destroy.

The True Vine is the legitimate God who wants you to live the genuine life of God in Him. He wants you to prosper and be in good spiritual, physical and mental health.

> Beloved, I pray that you may prosper in all things and be in health, just as your soul prospers. (3 John 2 NKJV)
>
> Dear friend, I hope all is well with you and that you are as healthy in body as you are strong in spirit. (3 John 2 NIV)

This all goes back to our life as healthy and vibrant branches that are connected to the True Vine.

Our heavenly Father is the owner of the garden. He cares for us, because we are the branches connected to the True Vine. We abide in Him and seek Him with our entire being. He provides and cares for us.

In our relationship with the True Vine and the Father, believers live in God's vineyard. We intentionally remain connected to the True Vine and receive our very life and existence from God.

As believers, we have a connected, fruitful life, one with God. We live with God and we hear from God. Similar to the believer's life with God is that of Moses and Joshua. Both of these individuals loved and obeyed God. They both abided in a permanent, genuine relationship with God and followed Him with their lives.

The apostle Paul's relationship with God changed. We first see Paul in Acts as a man that was devoted to the Law and who actively persecuted Christians. After his encounter with Jesus on the road to Damascus, he became a believer and followed Jesus. He was now connected to the True Vine. The same opportunity is there for believers. We become connected to Jesus the True Vine when we decide to receive Him as our Lord and live for Him. We are permanently joined to Him and tended to by the Father.

Like Paul being led by Jesus the True Vine, believers today are led by God. The scriptures teach that God is actively and intimately involved in our lives. Being connected with the True Vine and being cared for by the Father is more than a superficial connection – it is God's love in action as He cares for believers.

In closing, being connected to the True Vine is necessary for every believer. A relationship with Him is established when we are saved. We live eternally connected to Him. Today, live and abide in the True Vine.

Chapter Questions for Discussion or Study

1. Jesus, the True Vine, is genuine. He is not some imitation plastic vine. Why is this an essential truth for every believer?

2. How do "real" money and counterfeit money help us understand God?

3. Identify a "vine" that is a place that people choose instead of Jesus the True Vine. Why are these vines not good and do not honor God?

4. Why do people seek to replace God in their lives?

5. Unbelievers claim that there are many paths to God. Why is this untrue? Why is Jesus the only way to get to God?

6. FILL-IN: 3 John 2 NKJV - Beloved, I pray that you may _____ in all things and be in _____, just as your _____ prospers.

John 15
Chapter 2
God Loves Trees

God loves trees.

How do I know that God loves trees? He created the trees and plants in the garden and called His workmanship "good." If God is planting a garden, it is sure to be perfect and done right the first time!

> Then God said, "I give you every seed-bearing plant on the face of the whole earth and every tree that has fruit with seed in it. They will be yours for food. And to all the beasts of the earth and all the birds in the sky and all the creatures that move along the ground - everything that has the breath of life in it - I give every green plant for food." And it was so. God saw all that he had made, and it was very good. And there was evening, and there was morning - the sixth day. (Genesis 1:29-31 NIV)

> Now the LORD God had planted a garden in the east, in Eden; and there he put the man he had

formed. The LORD God made all kinds of trees grow out of the ground - trees that were pleasing to the eye and good for food. In the middle of the garden were the tree of life and the tree of the knowledge of good and evil. (Genesis 2:8-9 NIV)

When we talk about trees, we know that branches die if they are cut from the tree. If you cut off a branch from the tree it will not grow leaves, flowers won't blossom in the Spring and it definitely will not grow fruit. Unattached branches are doomed to die and wither. But branches attached to the tree will grow and bear fruit – that's what they do. Christians that stay attached and close in their relationship with God are fruitful. When believers follow God's directions and do what they are supposed to, they will grow and produce fruit. We're like a branch on a tree – we must stay attached to live as the healthy branch remains attached.

Like a forest of trees, the Father loves all of the branches in His vineyard – the vine and every branch. This is God's planting and He takes impeccable care. He clears away the dead branches and He prunes that which is productive.

> He cuts off every branch of mine that doesn't produce fruit, and he prunes the branches that do bear fruit so they will produce even more. (John 15:2 NLT)

The Father takes us and prunes us. His pruning is cutting away the dead unnecessary things in our lives. Some things He prunes are harmful to us, some are outright sin and some of the pruning are things that are a waste of our time, disrespectful to God and definitely do not glorify Him. This pruning helps the believer to grow stronger and more productive for God. The Father's pruning makes this growth possible.

When we read Psalm 1, it is more than just words. It is the inspired Word of God that tells us about the exciting life of the righteous and the tragic life of the wicked. It is important that the believer receive, absorb and hold onto these words. We follow God and are one of God's trees!

> Oh, the joys of those who do not follow the advice of the wicked, or stand around with sinners, or join in with mockers. But they delight in the law of the LORD, meditating on it day and night. They are like trees planted along the riverbank, bearing fruit each season. Their leaves never wither and they prosper in all they do. But not the

wicked! They are like worthless chaff, scattered by the wind. They will be condemned at the time of judgment. Sinners will have no place among the godly. For the LORD watches ever the path of the godly, but the path of the wicked leads to destruction. For the LORD watches over the way of the righteous, but the way of the wicked leads to destruction. (Psalm 1:1-6 NLT)

This Psalm paints an uplifting and beautiful picture of God's love for the righteous. The righteous believer is planted by God and produces fruit regularly. He loves the trees that He plants.

We see some important things about the righteous believers who God likens to trees.

- Sinners and those who mock God are not the companions of the righteous.
- God's trees are permanently planted alongside the river.
- They bear fruit and their leaves do not die.
- They are prosperous in everything.
- They are not like the wicked who God will judge.

A beautiful picture is painted in Psalm 1. God's trees are planted by the river and they look majestic with their leaves and fruit. The flowing river replenishes the trees and the trees prosper and grow. This prosperity tells me that the trees are in synch with God and fulfilling their purpose – to grow excellent fruit.

God's trees correspond with the True Vine and the branches. Every believer is a branch that is permanently attached to the True Vine. Like the trees that are planted by the river and produce fruit, so we are branches that receive their life from God through the True Vine. Believers produce fruit for God because of God. This is a promise to embrace - stay attached to God and produce fruit for God.

My grandparents had a grapevine on their farm. It was out next to the tractor shed by the pear tree. Grandmother used the grapes to make some of the best grape jelly ever! But the grapes were sour when you ate them. I am sure she added a lot of sugar when she made the jelly. The grapevine grew as my grandfather tended it. The grapevine was fulfilling its' God-ordained destiny - to grow and produce grapes. We fulfill our God-ordained destiny as we grow and prosper in the things of God and as we bear much fruit for Him.

Many years ago, my dad hung a swing for me at my grandparent's farm. It was hanging on the box elder tree that my grandfather had planted for my dad. When it was planted, it was a tiny sapling. But when I saw it, it was a huge tree. Because my grandfather cared for the box elder, it grew into a large tree. This is the family I came from – we nurture and care for plants and trees.

God nurtures and cares for the righteous people of His kingdom. Believers are like the tree carefully planted by the river where they will get sufficient water. He gives care and sees them come to bear fruit. God loves trees and He loves us.

My late friend Mike Williams gave me a Chinese dogwood tree several years ago. He had grown it from a seed and it was about one foot tall. It grew in my backyard into a beautiful flowering tree through nurture, pruning and care. It always made me think of my friend Mike.

My care for the Chinese dogwood tree from Mike helped me better understand God's love. In our lives, God waters and prunes us to bring forth fruit. This is a good lesson we can learn as we plant and grow trees, watch a farmer tend grapevines or plant a home garden.

When Jesus taught His disciples about the True Vine that evening, he talked about something they were familiar with. Vineyards were everywhere in Israel. All of these life processes bring a direct lesson about God that believers can and should learn. Believers can be assured that God will nurture you, prune you and help you grow.

One of the arborist websites asks a question, "Are your trees looking lifeless today? They may just need a good pruning." (Greentops.com) An arborist is an expert that knows all about trees and woody plants. God is an expert on tending the people He attached to the True Vine. We are the benefactors of His expert care because of His great love for each of us.

When I hear about God's pruning, I immediately shudder and think – "Am I next?" When I prune and cut back trees, I do not think about what the tree feels. When I become aware of God pruning me, it takes me a while to realize that even though it is not always a pleasant experience, God is an expert and in control. I often forget that God is perfect – no mistakes, no errors. His sole objective is to help me and make me able to grow more fruit.

We grow up being told the line that "this won't hurt!" It's an attempt to refocus you from the soon-coming pain. When God prunes believers, it often hurts us because our pride is "bruised." We ask "Why is this happening God?" I agree with His objectives and want His will. But it's not often easy. God prunes away unproductive things that stop or hinder our spiritual growth. As a believer, all I can say is "prune on Lord!"

We are His loved branches attached to the True Vine and under the Father's care. God's love for us becomes very evident when we focus on the real issue – His love. We are blessed as we think about His love and actively live it as branches and trees. Today consider and live His love. Let His love flow from the Father into your life and be changed.

Be blessed, and know that you are a cared-for branch attached to Jesus, the True Vine.

Chapter Questions for Discussion or Study

1. "If God is planting a garden, it is sure to be perfect and gets done right the first time!" Why is His garden perfect? How do we know His garden is perfect?

2. Branches die when they are cut from a tree. Why do believers suffer when they separate themselves from God?

3. Why does the Father prune dead things from our lives?

4. How does Psalm 1 help us understand more about God's love?

John 15 Chapter 3 We Are Growing Fruit

When we talk about the vine and the fruit, it is clear to us that growing fruit is the purpose of a vine. Vines are not like the bushes we planted in front of our house. The bushes are meant to be ornamental, making the house look beautiful. Grapevines are planted to bear fruit. Plant the vine, grow the grapes, harvest the grapes and produce the wine.

> Remain in me, as I also remain in you. No branch can bear fruit by itself; it must remain in the vine. Neither can you bear fruit unless you remain in me. (John 15:4 NIV)

When we consider our relationship with God and the truly important matters in our life, we know that He is the most important person in our lives. John 15 tells us that Jesus is the True Vine and the Father is the vinedresser (also called the husbandman), the farmer who tends the vines. Believers are the branches that are attached to the vine.

> I am the vine; you are the branches. If you remain in me and I in you, you will bear much fruit; apart from me you can do nothing. (John 15:5 NIV)

> I am the vine, ye are the branches: He that abideth in me, and I in him, the same bringeth forth much fruit: for without me ye can do nothing. (John 15:5 KJV)

The branch that abides in the vine <u>will</u> produce fruit. This is what the above scripture tells us, "you will bear much fruit." When the believer abides in the True Vine, they develop a living relationship of give and take. The branch receives nourishment from the vine and produces fruit.

Fruit is the product of this abiding relationship. The branch abides and receives everything from the vine needed to grow and produce fruit. As believers, we are the branches who remain permanently attached to Jesus the True Vine. A branch receives all of its nourishment and life from the vine and believers receive all of their nourishment and life from Jesus. Our relationship with Jesus is intended to be a "forever thing."

When an abiding branch produces fruit, the branch will fulfill it's purpose. Believers are called by God to abide in the True Vine and produce fruit. This is how we fulfill our purposes. He has the ability and the desire for every believer to grow frit. Jesus is doing this because it advances the Kingdom of God, brings glory to the Father and blesses His body, the Church.

An interesting fact in John 15 is that it teaches that there is a progressive increase of fruit from the branch. It goes from no fruit to some fruit to more fruit and ends with much fruit.

- People start with <u>no fruit</u>. Despite being a good or religious person, there is no fruit for God. This is because unbelievers do not produce fruit that glorifies the Father. They might do some good things, but fruit for God does not exist. No relationship, no fruit.
- The believer who is starting out begins by producing <u>some fruit</u>. This fruit brings glory and honor to the Father.
- God wants us to increase and produce <u>more fruit</u>. He wants us to bless and help more people. As believers produce more fruit, it brings praise and glory to our God.

- The last stage is <u>much fruit</u>. This is the goal and the permanent way of life for every believer. We are to grow and bring much fruit to God through all of the jobs and tasks that God sends each of us to do.

Every believer will produce unique fruit because every believer is unique - they are all sent by God to do different things. In the same way that no two believers are alike, no two ministries are alike. Everyone is called to the ministry of being a priest serving God. Some believers are called to formal ministry. Whatever your calling, all believers serve God within their calling.

> Some believers are called into special positions to serve Him.
>
> And [His gifts to the church were varied and] He Himself appointed some as apostles [special messengers, representatives], some as prophets [who speak a new message from God to the people], some as evangelists [who spread the good news of salvation], and some as pastors and teachers [to shepherd and guide and instruct], [and He did this] to fully equip *and* perfect the saints (God's people) for works of

service, to build up the body of Christ [the church]; (Ephesians 4:11-12 AMP)

These special leadership positions as ministers are designed to *equip and perfect* the saints. These words in Greek mean a *complete furnishing*. When we decide to redo our house, we paint, change the flooring, hang pictures on the wall and get some new furniture. We make it new and useful by doing certain things when we completely change and refurbish the room. God makes us useful by *thoroughly equipping* the believer.

As the minister brings and explains the Scriptures to us and the Holy Spirit makes them alive, God reveals His truths to us. These leadership ministers are charged with serving (ministering to) the saints. In carrying out this ministry, they "fully equip *and* perfect the saints (God's people) for works of service, to build up the body of Christ"

This training helps <u>every</u> believer grow fruit and become effective as they serve God. We are all ministers that serve God by loving and helping people. We preach the Good News – God loves you and wants you to come home to Him. When we work for God, we know we can be used by God because we have been thoroughly equipped and ready for action!

Every believer is connected to the True Vine. As we are one with Him, we will bear fruit. Trying to produce fruit in our own power will not work and we will fail. Despite our good intentions, kindness or faith, we will fail to produce fruit. It only works if we abide in Him and keep our relationship active.

> Remain in me, as I also remain in you. <u>No branch can bear fruit by itself</u>; it must remain in the vine. Neither can you bear fruit unless you remain in me. (John 15:4 NIV – underline added)

> I am the vine, ye are the branches: He that abideth in me, and I in him, the same bringeth forth much fruit: <u>for without me ye can do nothing.</u> (John 15:5 KJV – underline added)

Believers are not fruitful unless they abide in Jesus. All believers want to glorify God and serve Him. Abiding is an ongoing and eternal way of life for the believer. We never stop or interrupt the process - we abide permanently. When the believer gives diligent attention to our abiding, producing fruit for God is the result.

"Without me you can do nothing." An unbeliever cannot bear fruit for God. We are not independent but entirely dependent upon God. Our dependence is on us (a branch) being connected to the True Vine. Our life is only found in Him.

As the Father prunes us, our fruit increases in quality and quantity. The dead wood and unproductive areas in our lives have to be pruned (cut back) so we can use the life energy of the True Vine to increase and to grow a lot of fruit.

Pruning involves cutting away some things in our lives, which means change on our part. Change is not always easy and not always what we want. But pruning is necessary to help us grow more fruit. I am sure if the maple tree I trimmed back a few years ago could talk, it would have yelled "ouch!" and "stop!" when I cut it back. I cut it so much that I was sure I had killed it. But it came back twice as big as before. God prunes us for our good when He cuts away our failings, sin and harmful things to cause us to bear more fruit and become a more substantial branch on the vine.

We bear fruit for God in a variety of ways.

- The most obvious is the *Fruit of the Spirit*, which Paul wrote about in Galatians.
    > But the fruit of the Spirit is love, joy, peace, longsuffering, kindness, goodness, faithfulness, gentleness, and self-

control. Against such there is no law. (Galatians 5:22-23 NKJV)
- When believers win people to Christ, God attaches them to the True Vine.
    > The fruit of the righteous *is a* tree of life, And he who wins souls *is* wise. (Proverbs 11:30 NKJV)
- Bringing in the harvest of souls is a group effort of all believers. (John 4:35-38)
    > I tell you, open your eyes and look at the fields! They are ripe for harvest. (John 4:35b NIV)
- Growing in holiness to God. (The increase and consistency of obedience and holiness)
    > But now you are free from the power of sin and have become slaves of God. Now you do those things that lead to holiness and result in eternal life. (Romans 6:22 NLT)
- Being dedicated to God will take sacrifice.
    > Brothers and sisters, in view of all we have just shared about God's compassion, I encourage you to offer your bodies as living sacrifices, dedicated to God and

> pleasing to him. This kind of worship is appropriate for you. (Romans 12:1)

These are just a few examples of the fruit that we bring when we are totally connected with Jesus. Believers grow and bear fruit when we abide in the True Vine.

Chapter Questions for Discussion or Study

1. What is the purpose of the vine? What is the purpose of the True Vine?

2. FILL-IN: As believers, we are the _____ who remain permanently attached to _____ the True Vine.

3. What is necessary for the branch to receive nourishment from the vine? What is necessary for the believer to receive nourishment from the True Vine?

4. There is a progressive increase of the Fruit of the Spirit in the believer. What are the four steps of increase?

5. What is the reason that each believer produces UNIQUE fruit?

6. What is the job of every person called into special leadership?

7. How and why will the believer produce the Fruit of the Holy Spirit?

8. FILL-IN: _____ are not fruitful unless they abide in _____.

9. Why does God prune believers?

John 15
Chapter 4
Enabled By God

Being *enabled* by God is a GREAT thing. God's enablement means giving His authority or means to do something. God provides His authority through His Word and the name of Jesus and guides, guides, and helps us accomplish His will and desires. He enables and we cooperate with Him. In this relationship with the True Vine, we accomplish His goals.

> I am the vine; you are the branches. If you remain in me and I in you, you will bear much fruit; apart from me you can do nothing. If you do not remain in me, you are like a branch that is thrown away and withers; such branches are picked up, thrown into the fire and burned. If you remain in me and my words remain in you, ask whatever you wish, and it will be done for you. This is to my Father's glory, that you bear much fruit, showing yourselves to be my disciples. (John 15:5-8 NIV)

When God enables us, He gives us His authority, His provision and His power to carry out His wishes. His enabling makes us able to bear much fruit. Our responsibility is to cooperate – work together with Him.

God will not do everything for us. He tells us we must have faith to please Him, obey Him, forgive and love people, and live a life consistent with the Word of God.

God's *enablement* is always a good thing. He is a good God who blesses His people. He does what the right thing for us is. He will answer our prayers (v.7), but we must pray what is consistent with His Word. We can always trust His enabling because our perfect God has perfect love and He loves us forever.

What does *disable* mean? It means to stop or to be put out of action. We refer to a car that is broken down on the side of the road as a *disabled* vehicle.

In Bible times as well as today, people are disabled by the devil, by sin and by their own bad beliefs and attitudes. They are stopped by the devil's disabling. This disabling keeps people from coming to Jesus and receiving Him as Lord and Savior. We see the contrast between enabling and disabling in scripture.

> The thief comes only to steal and kill and destroy; I have come that they may have life, and have it to the full. (John 10:10 NIV)

> A thief is only there to disable as he steals, kills and destroys. I came so they can have real and eternal life, more and better life than they ever dreamed of. (John 10:10 MSG)

The thief disables us through our not believing in God and living a life of sin – he steals, kills and destroys. Jesus enables us with abundant life, righteousness and eternal life from God. The thief is the devil. Everything he does is sinful and evil and he steals from us. Jesus brought us eternal life which we receive through faith in Him. This is eternal life with God - the life from God that everyone needs.

When we talk about God enabling us, we need to know that the Holy Spirit is in our lives. The Holy Spirit of God is a spirit, not a human with a physical body. He is a person. Jesus referred to the Spirit as "He" and not "it." The Holy Spirit has a mind (Romans 8:27) and a will (1 Corinthians 12:11). He has emotional feelings (Galatians 5:22-23) which tells us that He expresses the love of God to us and has compassion in all He does.

When the Holy Spirit guides and helps us, He does not try something to see if it works. He has a definite plan and will carry it out. When the Holy Spirit enables us, He equips us with power for service. He provides the skills we need and we are "fueled" with His power so we can successfully and completely serve Him.

The contrast between enabled and disabled is also seen in the example shown in Matthew.

> Anyone who listens to my teaching and follows it is wise, like a person who builds a house on solid rock. Though the rain comes in torrents and the floodwaters rise and the winds beat against that house, it won't collapse because it is built on bedrock. But anyone who hears my teaching and doesn't obey it is foolish, like a person who builds a house on sand. When the rains and floods come and the winds beat against that house, it will collapse with a mighty crash. (Matthew 7:24-27 NLT)

One house is built on sand. Beach houses on the shore of the Atlantic Ocean are built with pilings driven down into the sandy ground. This is because standard building practices using a regular foundation are insufficient to keep the crashing waves from destroying the house.

When a massive ocean storm hits the house in Matthew 7, it collapsed with a mighty crash. This description speaks of the destructive nature of the storm and the bad decisions that were made when the owner built the house.

The other house is built on a rock. When a house is built on a rock, they use construction methods to firmly attach it to the rock. They drill holes and drive metal pins directly into the rocks. The scriptures said that this technique of pinning the house to the rock makes absolute sense – it shows wisdom in the design. This is why it is crucial to build a house following good construction techniques. To state it plainly, building on the sand is a dumb choice and building on a rock is a smart choice.

The house built on sand represents someone who has been disabled and the house on the rock represents an enabled person. We make choices when we make decisions – poor choices and wise choices. Poorly built houses collapse in a storm and are destroyed. Wisely built homes endure the high winds, the storm surge and flooding and remain where they are built.

> These words I speak to you are not incidental additions to your life, homeowner improvements to your standard of living. They are foundational

words, words to build a life on. If you work these words into your life, you are like a smart carpenter who built his house on solid rock. Rain poured down, the river flooded, a tornado hit—but nothing moved that house. It was fixed to the rock. But if you just use my words in Bible studies and don't work them into your life, you are like a stupid carpenter who built his house on the sandy beach. When a storm rolled in and the waves came up, it collapsed like a house of cards. (Matthew 7:24-27 MSG)

Even though we are talking about building a house, the real discussion here is trusting God through the teachings of Jesus – obeying and doing what the Bible teaches. I do this through reading, obeying and actively living what the Bible teaches. I do this through talking to God. I do this through following the leading and guiding of the Holy Spirit. I do this through having a trusting relationship with God.

We are taught in John 15 that a Christian lives and abides in the True Vine. Doing this enables a believer to receive from God. This connection brings us a permanent relationship with God which can result in making wise decisions that God reveals. These revelations come through His Word (the Bible) and the leading of the Holy Spirit. The enabled builder used God's wisdom and decided to do the right thing – build the house upon an immovable foundation. Believers use God's wise decisions in shaping and living their lives. Disablement causes people to wander aimlessly without God and follow their own thinking or the lies and deception of the devil and misguided people.

Believers choose to receive God's enabling when they reject and leave the disabling of the devil.

This comes down to making choices "God choices." I choose to be enabled and stay actively connected with the True Vine. I choose to receive the loving care of the Father. I choose to live my life with God through Jesus Christ.

Make the choice today to be enabled by abiding in the True Vine, Jesus Christ and receive the care of the Father.

Chapter Questions for Discussion or Study

1. FILL-IN: John 15:1 NIV - I am the _____ and you are the _____.

2. What does God give the believer when He enables us?

3. FILL-IN: John 10:10 NIV - The _____ comes only to _____ and _____ and _____; I have come that they may have _____, and have it to the _____.

4. Who is the thief who steal, kills and destroys? Why does the thief attack the believer?

5. Why does God enable the believer?

6. Why does the parable of the house on the rock and the sand help us understand God enabling us and us following God?

7. FILL-IN: Even though we are talking about building a _____, the real discussion here is obeying God through the teachings of _____ – obeying and doing what the _____ teaches.

John 15
Chapter 5
Abide In My Love

We saw that the word *abide* in John 15 means to settle down and remain. In addition, it comes with a sense of permanence. *Abide* does not describe a short-term encounter like meeting someone for a cup of coffee. Rather, it indicates a long-term relationship. A stray dog runs across the yard but your pet dog *abides* with you for a number of years. We may rent a hotel room, but we *abide* in our home or apartment.

Jesus explained that His love for <u>each</u> of us is like the love the Father has for Him. We will always *abide* in His love.

> As the Father loved Me, I also have loved you; abide in My love. (John 15:9 NKJV)

The Father has always loved Jesus and will love Him forever. This love is very apparent in the Gospels. Jesus and the Father have an amazing, close and totally unmatchable relationship. This is because Jesus takes the love of the Father and carries it to each of us. The Father loves Jesus and Jesus loves His Body, the Church. We permanently settle down (*abide*) in that love.

Jesus brings the Father's love to all people in His sacrifice.

> For God so loved the world that he gave his one and only Son, that whoever believes in him shall not perish but have eternal life. For God did not send his Son into the world to condemn the world, but to save the world through him. (John 3:16-17 NIV)

This love is available to all people. The true meaning of this love was defined by the Father when He sent Jesus to die. This is what we abide in – His love which is actually a *greater* love.

> Greater love has no one than this, than to lay down one's life for his friends. (John 15:13 NKJV)

The Father sent Jesus to bring this greater love in Jesus' death, burial, resurrection and eternal life. This is what we abide in – His greater love. We will examine His greater love in the next chapter.

The disciples were people who were learning to understand the words of Jesus – "abide in My love." They were with Him for about 3 ½ years. They embraced the love of the Father through Jesus and saw great value in this permanent relationship. On one occasion, the disciples were asked by Jesus if they would continue to follow Him and Peter gave the disciples' answer to Jesus.

> Simon Peter answered him, "Lord, to whom shall we go? You have the words of eternal life, and we have believed, and have come to know, that you are the Holy One of God." (John 6:68-69 ESV)

Peter was telling Jesus "there is nowhere else that we can go." Jesus had already brought the disciples into a relationship with Him and wanted to know if <u>they</u> would continue.

- Jesus had taught them about eternal life with God.
- The disciples received His words and accepted them.
- God revealed to the disciples that Jesus was the Messiah.

The disciples clearly show believers today that abiding in His love is the only smart way to live our lives. Jesus said "abide in My love." Jesus is reaching out to each of us and telling us that He is the only one we can trust. Our lives are valuable to Him and we are safe because we trust in Jesus.

When believers abide in His love, they have a totally dependable connection with God through Jesus Christ. This connection causes us to depend upon Him as we live our lives. Think about this wonderful thing – He reaches out to us, we respond and He brings all of the Kingdom of God to bear in our lives.

What if someone does not abide in His love? They have never made a choice to follow Jesus. This makes them an unbeliever – people who do not believe. They might like the idea of following God. They cannot be saved until someone believes in their heart that God raised Jesus from the dead and receives the forgiveness He provides. They cannot abide in His love.

Abiding in His love involves having and nurturing an ongoing relationship with Jesus. In this relationship, the believer grows in God. The Scriptures clearly teach that abiding consists in being active in His Word.

> If you abide in Me, and My words abide in you, you will ask what you desire, and it shall be done for you. (John 15:7 NKJV)

This abiding relationship is more than telling God "I need this or "I want that." When we abide in His love, our mutual relationship is one of His Lordship, His friendship and walking with God. This is abiding in His love.

O Love of God is an old and famous song that tells us how His love really blesses us. The lyrics below are a fantastic description of this love.

> O love of God, how rich and pure! How measureless and strong! It shall forevermore endure, the saints and angels' song.

This is the love which we abide in – the life of a believer is one of us being an active part of His love.

An interesting question is "what if we wander away from God?" We see this in the life of the apostle Peter. Peter had a relationship with Jesus and he abided in His love. Later, he denied Jesus hours before His crucifixion. Even though Peter abandoned Him, Jesus sought Peter after the resurrection and restored Him. He told Peter to "feed My sheep." Jesus was telling Peter to get active and serve Him through doing what he was called to do. Peter was a central part of spreading the good news starting on the day of Pentecost (Acts 2).

When we wander away, Jesus loves us, pursues us and restores us to Him. We return to Him and return to actively abiding in His love again. We saw this in Peter's life and it is true today in the life of a believer. This is abiding in the love of God.

Abiding in His love equips us for service. In Acts 2, the believers were together with one purpose. The Holy Spirit came and He equipped them for service. They were empowered and emboldened by the Holy Spirit. The believers were changed and ready to go. Jesus told them to bring the Gospel to everyone everywhere. Now they could do it.

Peter preached that day to the Jews who had gathered in response to the commotion caused by the coming of the Holy Spirit.

> Then Peter stood up with the eleven, raised his voice and addressed the crowd (Acts 2:14a NIV)

The Lord knew that this was what the believers needed – the presence and power of His Spirit. They now had God with them! The disciples could now go and preach the Gospel. They could go and heal people and free them from the devil. They could go and bring new life to people.

We serve God and we have this same power that Jesus had. This is because we have the same Holy Spirit.

> Jesus Christ *is* the same yesterday, today, and forever. (Hebrews 13:8 NKJV)

> For Jesus doesn't change—yesterday, today, tomorrow, he's always totally himself. (Hebrews 13:8 MSG)

The scriptures teach that Jesus Christ never changes – He saves, heals and raises the dead, both then and now. I think of this as Jesus intervening in our lives in the past, 24/7 now and for eternity. This is a truly great blessing that shows God's love for us.

When we abide in His love, we experience Jesus' full presence in our lives. We no longer live independently of God, but are now totally dependent upon God. Believers are followers of God and no longer those who ignore and deny God. We embrace, not refuse God.

Abide in His love today.

Chapter Questions for Discussion or Study

1. What does the word *abide* mean? Why is this a good description of our relationship with God?

2. Why is *abiding* a permanent relationship?

3. FILL-IN: John 15:13 NKJV - _____ love has no one than this, than to lay down one's _____ for his friends.

4. Why is abiding in His love is the only smart way to live our lives?

5. We abide in Jesus and live permanently in Him. Why is this important for the believer?

6. FILL-IN: We serve God and we have this same power that _____ had. This is because we have the same _____ Spirit.

7. FILL-IN: Hebrews 13:8 – Jesus Christ is the same _____, _____ and forever.

8. Explain why Hebrews 13:8 is essential for the believer to know and live.

John 15
Chapter 6
Greater Love

Jesus' love for all people is greater because it extends to everyone and meets the need for love in our lives. But what should we know about this *greater love*? The scripture in John 15 tells us.

> Greater love has no one than this, than to lay down one's life for his friends. (John 15:13 NKJV)

> This is the very best way to love. Put your life on the line for your friends. (John 15:13 MSG)

In Greek, *greater* means numerous, large and abundant. This definition speaks to a greater quantity that is more effective.

God's love is easy to see when we understand that God is perfect, all-powerful and eternal. God comes down to our level with greater love and meets our need for salvation and a relationship with Him. The human race was and is a mess and that's why Jesus willingly gave Himself to save us.

God had a plan to rescue the world. Jesus was fully cooperating with the Father and the Holy Spirit. Jesus carried out God's will. He was not helpless at the hands of the hateful religious leaders or the Roman government. Jesus was not following God with a fear of the unknown, but He had faith in the plan of God. This is His *greater* love.

When Jesus surrendered His life for His friends, His love went far above human friendship. Jesus showed loyalty and concern and taught us more when He spoke about God's love for us. There was no "cheap talk" from Jesus. His friendship with us was motivated by His greater love.

This greater love is still available today. Believers tell people that "Jesus loves you!" This is more than a religious cliche or slogan. He spoke of His love and confirmed it by allowing Himself to be mercilessly crucified – a slow death on a cross. His resurrection and return to God followed this. This is the *greater* love of God in action.

When believers bring the good news of Christ's death, burial and resurrection to "all of the world," we carry His greater love. His greater love brought Him willingly to die on the cross. It is this same love today that motivates believers to dedicate themselves to the mission of the Gospel. The Church cooperates with the Holy Spirit and serves Christ as we bring His greater love to people.

As His greater love for people brought Him to the cross, His greater love brings God's plan and mission to pass today. The scope and size of His mission changed and became much more extensive. The next aspect of His greater love went into effect in Acts 2.

Before the resurrection, Jesus worked with His 12 disciples. They would travel from town to town while Jesus preached, healed and delivered people. After the resurrection, He sent His disciples to the entire world to fulfill His mission.

> And then he told them, "Go into all the world and preach the Good News to everyone. Anyone who believes and is baptized will be saved. But anyone who refuses to believe will be condemned. These miraculous signs will accompany those who believe: They will cast out demons in my name, and they will speak in new languages. They will be able to handle snakes with safety, and if they drink anything poisonous, it won't hurt them. They will be able to

> place their hands on the sick, and they will be healed." (Mark 16:15-18 NLT)

This scripture describes what they were to do – bring salvation, cast out demons, speak in new tongues, resist death by His power and bring God's healing to those who are sick. This is bringing the Gospel to people.

The book of Acts tells us that there were about 120 people who were gathered together when God sent the Holy Spirit to the believers. What did they do? The disciples went out and explained that the Holy Spirit had come (Acts 2). Peter preached Jesus the Messiah to the people in the street. There were about 3,000 people "who gladly received his [Peter's] word were baptized" into Christ. This was the first significant event for the Church! All of this happened because of the power and authority of the Holy Spirit was given to the people of God.

Jesus had a greater love for these people who needed God. The Holy Spirit empowered Peter and the disciples to bring God's message and the people were strongly convinced by the Holy Spirit to change the course of their lives and believe in Jesus Christ.

> "So let everyone in Israel know for certain that God has made this Jesus, whom you crucified, to be both Lord and

Messiah!" Peter's words pierced their hearts, and they said to him and to the other apostles, "Brothers, what should we do?" Peter replied, "Each of you must repent of your sins and turn to God, and be baptized in the name of Jesus Christ for the forgiveness of your sins. Then you will receive the gift of the Holy Spirit. This promise is to you, to your children, and to those far away - all who have been called by the Lord our God." (Acts 2:36-39 NLT)

Repentance by these people resulted in their salvation. The people became believers through this simple but profound decision and action.

This is still the case today. Unbelievers repent and decide to believe in Jesus. His greater love redeems them and welcomes them into God's Kingdom.

The greater love of Jesus is easy to understand, mainly because God is love. The greater love of Jesus is revealed in the greatness of God - in everything thing He is and everything He does. Believers have eternal life today because of this greater love.

How does all of this relate to me as a believer? We carry His love and give it to people. Believers believe in God and live for God. We bring an understanding of the greater love of Christ to people and the Holy Spirit draws them to His love.

> Then Christ will make his home in your hearts as you trust in him. Your roots will grow down into God's love and keep you strong. And may you have the power to understand, as all God's people should, how wide, how long, how high, and how deep his love is. May you experience the love of Christ, though it is too great to understand fully. Then you will be made complete with all the fullness of life and power that comes from God. (Ephesians 3:17-19 NLT)

Believers pray for people and with people. You might be the one person God will use to help someone find God. This is the greater love of Jesus in action.

In closing, men, women and children have the opportunity to know, experience and bring the greater love of God to people. This is a beautiful thing that Jesus Christ has given us as believers. Thank God for the greater love of Jesus Christ.

Chapter Questions for Discussion or Study

1. What was God's plan to rescue the human race? How was He successful?

2. Why is it crucial that a believer find, obey and do God's plan for their life?

3. Jesus willingly surrendered and gave His life for us. How is a believer to give his life away?

4. What does the word *greater* mean? How does this definition help you to understand John 15:13 NKJV better?

5. How do believers carry this greater love to people when we preach the gospel to them?

6. FILL-IN: His friendship with us was motivated by His greater _____.

7. Jesus calls every believer his friend. How does His friendship with Him make a believer different from unbelievers?

8. We carry His love and give it to people. Believers believe in God and live for God. We bring an understanding of the greater love of Christ to people and the

Holy Spirit draws them to His love. How does this relate to every believer?

John 15

Chapter 7

Appointed To Bear Fruit

Jesus told us to bear fruit. He did not say, "I hope you bear fruit" or maybe "If everything is just right, you might get lucky and bear a few pieces of fruit" or "someday when you're good enough, the fruit will come."

> Ye have not chosen me, but I have chosen you, and ordained you, that ye should go and bring forth fruit, and that your fruit should remain: that whatsoever ye shall ask of the Father in my name, he may give it you. (John 15:16 KJV)

> You didn't choose me, remember; I chose you, and put you in the world to bear fruit, fruit that won't spoil. As fruit bearers, whatever you ask the Father in relation to me, he gives you. (John 15:16 MSG)

The KJV says we were *chosen* and *ordained* to bear fruit. *Chosen* tells us that we were picked out. When I was young, I was quickly picked when we played football. With other sports, not so much. I was *chosen* to serve in a role on the team. For me it was using my size and strength to block and tackle people.

Jesus picked every believer to produce fruit that will glorify Him, to bless and help other people and fulfill what He wants in our lives. *Ordained* is a similar word, that shows Jesus placing us so that we will successfully serve Him. I was *ordained* as a football player to block and tackle those people – it was my mission.

The church ordains ministers to serve God, His church and His people. God chooses and ordains people to serve Him and bear fruit. The life of a believer should be one of producing fruit that lasts. We permanently abide in the True Vine and always continue to produce permanent fruit.

Jesus said that trees will be recognized as good or bad – good trees mean good fruit and bad trees mean bad fruit.

> Thus, by their fruit you will recognize them. (Matthew 7:20 NIV)

A *good* tree is valuable and virtuous. A believer is immediately made righteous, valuable and virtuous through faith in Jesus Christ. Because we are a *good* tree, we produce *good* fruit as a normal, everyday way of life. Righteous believers produce fruit that is consistent with God's standards.

The Church is sent and empowered by God to produce fruit. God gives this fruit through believers to people who need the fruit. This fruit is to bless people and provide for their needs.

We can see this fruit in Galatians 5. This is the fruit we are appointed to bear.

> But the Holy Spirit produces this fruit in our lives: love, joy, peace, patience, kindness, goodness,
> faithfulness, gentleness, and self-control. There is no law against these things! (Galatians 5:22-23 NLT)

We abide in the True Vine with a permanent relationship with God. The Holy Spirit changes our lives and we serve God. In our new righteous lives, we produce fruit that remains.

- <u>Believers have a love</u> for God and love for others. We serve a God of love – God is love! Having

the love of God is the thing that makes Christians different.
- <u>The joy</u> that comes from God is within us and it is exciting. We spread that joy to other people. We can freely "pour" joy out on others through the Holy Spirit! Remember, you can have a problem or challenge in your life and still overflow with God's joy.
- <u>Peace</u> from God goes beyond human reason, logic or understanding. Jesus brings us His peace and we bring it to others. We live confident, knowing He will care for us. His peace transcends everything on this earth.
- <u>Patience</u> is called longsuffering in the KJV. We continue to do God's will regardless of the cost or the opposition we receive. We patiently endure and GO FORWARD! God's patience tells us He is for us. Regardless of who tries to stop us from serving God, He will cause us to be successful and triumphantly serve Him.

- <u>Kindness</u> is being good to people regardless of their actions. A gentle reaction to others is good. A rude, mean and harsh attitude is not the believers' way. We follow Jesus spoke very direct and strong and used self-control with all people. We draw people <u>to God</u> with the fruit of kindness.
- <u>Goodness</u> is acting and living through our renewed and righteous self. As followers of Jesus, we do *good* things. Our *good* actions speak volumes – they tell people we know and trust God. We bring *this goodness* to others. It is much more than words. It's a believer acting out and doing the will of God.
- <u>Faithfulness</u> shows our loyalty to God and our loyalty to people. Jesus did what He said He would do. He didn't forget to do something or find it inconvenient – He always loved, helped, etc. He was *faithful* to God and bought our salvation by giving His life. This is the call to each

believer - be faithful to God and give yourself away to others as Jesus did. We can be faithful to God. God is always faithful and we should also be faithful.
- <u>Gentleness</u> is mild or meek behavior. Meek does not mean wimpy or weak. Moses was meek and humble, yet he showed strength to Pharaoh and the Israelite people. Moses was always gentle and meek to God. This is how we should be to God and people.
- <u>Self-control</u> is mastering desires and passions, allowing the godly desires, and stopping the desires that oppose God – sin, evil, etc.

Believers live a life where the Fruit of the Spirit is produced by faith, and only occurs as we abide in the True Vine. We produce lasting fruit because we abide in Jesus, the True Vine.

We have to exhibit self-control. Always. But when we trust God and work together with Him, He brings His power. When we cooperate (work together) with Him fruit is produced. The Father takes care of us, the life comes from the True Vine and we produce fruit. This is normal, everyday Christian living.

I have found that as I work <u>with</u> God, as I bow my knee to Him and obey – I am blessed with His presence and His Fruit comes naturally. I agree with Him and He blesses me. I can be a blessing to the people I come in contact with. An example of this is found in loving God. God loved us and we love Him. As we come in contact with others, we spread the love of God. We are carriers "infected" with His love. We are "contagious" and become active givers of His love.

> We love Him because He first loved us. (1 John 4:19 NKJV)

> Believers are going to love and be loved. First, we were loved and now we love. He loved us first. (1 John 4:19 MSG)

I love God and He loves me. Because of His great and generous love, I want to love others. Some people are in tremendous need of love, some are down and out and some are surrounded by tragedy. Believers and the lost need His love. This is the Fruit of the Spirit in action - God's love through each believer. It is easy and natural to love when the Holy Spirit works in your life, as we abide in Jesus, the True Vine.

We are appointed to be fruitful in service to God. Jesus sends us out to serve Him.

> Just as you sent me into the world, I am sending them into the world. (John 17:18 NLT)

God sent Jesus and He produced good fruit for God. He sends us to do the same.

We believe in Him and we receive eternal life from God. With our new eternal life and a relationship with God, we take the Good News and give it to other people – people who desperately need God in their lives. The Fruit of the Spirit proceeds from His Body, the Church. God Himself is brought to people by the power of the Holy Spirit through believers like you and I.

Jesus sent His disciples out to carry His good news to people.

> Jesus called his twelve disciples to him and gave them authority to drive out impure spirits and to heal every disease and sickness. (Matthew 10:1 NIV)

> The Lord now chose seventy-two other disciples and sent them ahead in pairs to all the towns and places he planned to visit. (Luke 10:1 NLT)

> Heal the sick, and tell them, 'The Kingdom of God is near you now.' (Luke 10:9 NLT)

Believers are sent out today, like the disciples were sent out. Believers produce fruit – the good news is preached, demons are cast out of people, the sick are healed and the kingdom of God is brought to people. The end result is changed lives. People are changed from a life of hopelessness and tragedy to a life of God's redemption and blessings.

Like His disciples, believers today are told to go and proclaim the good news to everyone.

> And He said to them, "Go into all the world and preach the gospel to all creation. (Mark 16:15 AMP)

You have been appointed to do this and bear fruit. Are you doing this with your life, your time and your resources? Today, accept and actively follow your personal appointment from God. Allow the Holy Spirit to work in and through you as you abide in the True Vine, Jesus Christ.

Chapter Questions for Discussion or Study

1. FILL-IN: John 15:16 MSG - You didn't _____ me, remember; I _____ you, and put you in the world to bear _____, fruit that won't _____. As fruit

bearers, whatever you _____ the Father in relation to me, he gives you.

2. FILL-IN: The KJV says we were _____ and _____ to bear fruit.

3. Jesus said that trees will be recognized as good or bad – good trees mean good fruit and bad trees mean bad fruit. What is an example of the Fruit we produce because of the Holy Spirit? How does this help people?

4. Because a believer is a *good* tree, we produce *good* fruit as a normal, everyday way of life. Identify one Fruit of the Spirit and explain how a believer serves God with this Fruit.

5. What is the Fruit of the Spirit? (Galatians 5:22-23)

6. FILL-IN: <u>Faithfulness</u> shows our loyalty to _____ and our loyalty to _____.

7. Why is Self-Control important for the believer?

8. As I work with God I am blessed. How has blessed you when you cooperate with Him?

9. God sent Jesus and He produced good fruit for God. He sends us to do the same. How does a believer produce good fruit that changes the lives of people?

10. Jesus sent His disciples out to carry His good news to people. What things can a believer do to bring His good news to people?

11. FILL-IN: Mark 16:15 AMP - And He said to them, "Go into all the _____ and preach the _____ to all creation.

John 15
Chapter 8
They Hated Me

Jesus tells us that the people of the world were haters - "they hated Me." Because Jesus is the Lord of your life, they will hate you too.

> If the world hates you, you know that it hated Me before *it hated* you. If you were of the world, the world would love its own. Yet because you are not of the world, but I chose you out of the world, therefore the world hates you. Remember the word that I said to you, 'A servant is not greater than his master.' If they persecuted Me, they will also persecute you. If they kept My word, they will keep yours also. But all these things they will do to you for My name's sake, because they do not know Him who sent Me. (John 15:18-21 NKJV)

> If you find the godless world is hating you, remember it got its start hating me. If you lived on the world's terms, the world would love you as one of its own.

> But since I picked you to live on God's terms and no longer on the world's terms, the world is going to hate you. When that happens, remember this: Servants don't get better treatment than their masters. If they beat on me, they will certainly beat on you. If they did what I told them, they will do what you tell them. (John 15:18-20 MSG)

The religious leaders hated Jesus and they loved their own religious beliefs more than they loved God. They chose to follow a manmade religion, not God. The religious leaders had defined and established their own rules and regulations outside of what the Word of God teaches. The Law and the prophets (the Old Testament) made unambiguous statements about God. These religious leaders had added their interpretations and applications and developed their own new and different way of having a relationship with God. The leaders modified the Law and the prophets and made it unrecognizable from the original word that came from God. They thought "we are serving God" but were opposing Him. This new so-called relationship with God was not good. This is one reason that Jesus was sent to the lost sheep of Israel - they had stopped following God.

> Jesus sent out the twelve apostles with these instructions: Don't go to the Gentiles or the Samaritans, but only to the people of Israel—God's lost sheep. Go and announce to them that the Kingdom of Heaven is near. Heal the sick, raise the dead, cure those with leprosy, and cast out demons. Give as freely as you have received! (Matthew 10:5-8 NLT)

Jesus came to show the truth to people – God loves you, He's not mad at you, so please come home to <u>your</u> God. Jesus brought this message from God to people and sent the disciples to carry that same message.

These people hated Jesus even though He was the Son of God as well as the Way, the Truth and the Life (John 14:6) He is Master, Messiah, Teacher and Lord over everyone and everything! He was sent by God and yet many rejected Him. This rejection of Jesus remains the choice of many today.

Jesus (the Truth of God) threatened their system, their power base and their money. He challenged their worldview to choose a new way of seeing things. Jesus was saying, "choose God."

What makes a believer different from the world and these rejectors and haters of God? We belong to God, not the "local haters club." We serve a God of love and we bring a message of love to the people of the world.

Believers will always be hated because they represent God and because people reject and oppose God's love in their lives. Jesus called us the "salt of the earth." (Matthew 5:13 NIV) Salt adds a unique seasoning to food. It also preserves food. Believers change people's lives by bringing change and preservation for eternity.

Believers are the "light of the world." (Matthew 5:14 NIV) We carry God's light to people and they resent His light. People's lives are exposed and lay open before God. Light invades the darkness and allows people to see the truth of God.

This brings us back to the fact that we belong to God. We do not belong to the world. I am deeply thankful that I belong to Him. Belonging to God is possible because He loved us first.

God calls all people to Him because He desires them to come to Him.

> The [Holy] Spirit and the bride (the church, believers) say, "Come." And let the one who hears say, "Come." And let the one who is thirsty come; let the one who wishes take *and* drink the water of

> life without cost. (Revelation 22:27 AMP)

People continually refuse God. They are offered a life from God without cost, yet they say "NO!" and "it's not for me." People will say "I'm not religious" or "there is no God." They satisfy their need for God with something else, often anything else! They will not acknowledge their condition and they do nothing.

Jesus is hated and believers are hated. But believers must not retaliate and become haters. We must actively live and continue to live in the love of God.

> When they hurled their insults at him, he did not retaliate; when he suffered, he made no threats. Instead, he entrusted himself to him who judges justly. (1 Peter 2:23 NIV)

> While being reviled *and* insulted, He did not revile *or* insult in return; while suffering, He made no threats [of vengeance], but kept entrusting *Himself* to Him who judges fairly. (1 Peter 2:23 AMP)

Jesus chose to trust God. He <u>did not</u> take matters into His own hands. He chose to exercise faith in God despite being hated and ignored.

> He was despised and rejected - a man of sorrows, acquainted with deepest grief. We turned our backs on him and looked the other way. He was despised, and we did not care. (Isaiah 53:3 NLT)

When a believer is persecuted, ostracized and rejected by the world, they must run to God and fellow believers for help. Believers must have relationships and fellowship with God and other believers. The importance of attending church and developing relationships with Christians is crucial. We are the Church, the Body of Christ, not independent contractors. We rely on God and His people for support, prayer, relationships and love. Jesus uses His people to care for people's needs.

Many of the early Christian martyrs in Rome accepted their persecution with a solid resolve to trust God. They were martyred because they would not renounce Christ and worship the Roman gods as well as worship and swear allegiance to the Roman Emperor. Their King was Jesus and they followed God. This loyalty to God resulted in their execution by various means, often being killed in the arena for show. They understood that they were being persecuted because the world hated God.

The Bible teaches that believers must allow God to take care of the haters. He will avenge the injustice and bring justice. Besides, the haters might just come to repentance.

> Dear friends, never take revenge. Leave that to the righteous anger of God. For the Scriptures say, "I will take revenge; I will pay them back," says the Lord. (Romans 12:19 NLT)

> Beloved, never avenge yourselves, but leave the way open for God's wrath [and His judicial righteousness]; for it is written [in Scripture], "VENGEANCE IS MINE, I WILL REPAY," says the Lord. (Romans 12:19 AMP)

One commentator said, "Stand aside yourself as a mere spectator, and let the wrath of God have free course to accomplish itself as He shall think well." (Ellicott) I have learned to "stand aside" and let God carry out His plan. Moses did this at the Red Sea and God destroyed the Egyptian army.

> Moses answered the people, "Do not be afraid. Stand firm and you will see the deliverance the LORD will bring you today. The Egyptians you see today you will never see again. (Exodus 14:13 NIV)

Whether it is a big or small issue - a "Red Sea moment" or a minor problem in the parking lot, believers must be calm, trust God in faith and let Him resolve the issue. This is not passivity on the part of the believer, but an active, living trust in God.

Jesus came knowing they would hate Him. He wanted them to accept and receive God. And have an abundant life with God. Instead, people chose the devil (John 10:10) The haters followed the devil and lived a life of destruction. The religious leaders persecuted Jesus to cause Him to suffer. But God brought good out of it – our salvation and eternity with God.

God will turn the problem of hatred into a blessing of good. He completely overpowers, reverses the bad things, and brings good out of the situation.

> And we know [with great confidence] that God [who is deeply concerned about us] causes all things to work together [as a plan] for good for those who love God, to those who are called according to His plan and purpose. (Romans 8:28 AMP)

Things might get challenging and tough, but God <u>will</u> always triumph.

In closing, we know that Christ came to do the works of God, and people hated Him. Because every believer is a child of God, people will hate you as you love and serve God. But Jesus told us to be cheerful in God, because He has overcome the world. As we trust God, we live in His overcoming! Trust in Christ today!

Chapter Questions for Discussion or Study

1. FILL-IN: John 15:18 NKJV - If the world hates you, you know that it _____ Me before it _____ you.

2. Why did the religious leaders hate Jesus? Why do people hate believers?

3. Why was Jesus sent to the lost sheep of Israel?

4. Jesus came to tell people that God loves them personally. Why is this an important message for people to hear?

5. People reject God in their lives. How do they try to fill their lives with something else besides God? What is their "go-to" when they avoid God?

6. When believers are hated, they must not retaliate. Why is this so? What should

believers do instead of trying to fight the hate?

7. FILL-IN: The Bible teaches that believers must allow _____ to take care of the haters.

8. One commentator said, "Stand aside yourself as a mere spectator, and let the wrath of God have free course to accomplish itself as He shall think well." How will God enable the believer to do this?

John 15

Chapter 9

Written In Their Law

Jesus told His disciples that He was hated for no reason. The haters had a distorted view of God's Law.

> This fulfills what is written in their Scriptures: "They hated me without cause." (John 15:25 NLT)
>
> Let them not rejoice over me who are wrongfully my enemies; Nor let them wink with the eye who hate me without a cause. (Psalm 35:19 NKJV)

This tells us that their law was not God's Law. The haters created their own law. Their hatred of Christ was based on what they believed from their religious rules, not on the holy Word of God. We are told to desire God's pure spiritual milk." This means we desire and receive God's word, not man's word.

> as newborn babes, desire the pure milk of the word, that you may grow thereby (1 Peter 2:2 NKJV)

> Like newborn babies, you must crave pure spiritual milk so that you will grow into a full experience of salvation. Cry out for this nourishment (1 Peter 2:2 NLT)

The haters probably knew the pure Word of God at one time. Instead of following God's Law, they changed their allegiance to their own interpretation of their law. They took their new beliefs (which were man-created) and made them a part of <u>their</u> religious beliefs. God did not inspire their law. The religious leaders created it to satisfy their needs for prestige, keeping their power and authority and their love for money. Their law misinterpreted and misapplied the Scriptures.

The righteous have a simple, God-inspired answer – following God and His Word. This is seen in the words of the prophet Isaiah.

> If you are willing and obedient, you will eat the good things of the land; (Isaiah 1:19 NIV)

> If you are willing and obedient, You shall eat the best of the land; (Isaiah 1:18 AMP)

Believers choose to follow the Bible and the direction of God willingly. We do this through obedience to God. When the believer follows God, God blesses them.

This prophetic statement from Isaiah relates closely to John 10:10b. Jesus explains that He came to give people a full life, one He calls an abundant life. Not an easy, uneventful life, but a satisfying life of following and living for God. Believers follow and enthusiastically live the Word of God - His scriptures.

Jesus the Messiah accurately followed God's Law. The Father's will became Jesus' will. God's desires were written upon Jesus' heart.

> Then I said, "Here I am, I have come - it is written about me in the scroll. I desire to do your will, my God; your law is within my heart." (Psalm 40:7-8 NIV)

Jesus came to do the will of God, not to follow the distorted law of man. The Law and the Prophets made it clear. When we follow His Law, we accept the revelation of abiding in the True Vine. When believers purpose in their hearts to follow Jesus, they will do the will of God. This is found in a sincere relationship with Him and not following man-established laws and dictates.

Their interpretations and traditions were useless. Their law did not have the powerful, God-centered effect of His Law. Their law was mere words and ideas. It did not come from God.

> Now, Israel, hear the decrees and laws I am about to teach you. Follow them so that you may live and may go in and take possession of the land the LORD, the God of your ancestors, is giving you. Do not add to what I command you and do not subtract from it, but keep the commands of the LORD your God that I give you. Deut 4:2 NIV)

This tells us to obey and do His laws and not to add our own private interpretations. Believers are to follow and preach the Word of God.

The best course of action is to believe God ahead of time and change if your beliefs are wrong.

> I will run the course of Your commandments, For you shall enlarge my heart. (Psalm 199:32 NKJV)

> I grasp and cling to whatever you tell me; GOD, don't let me down! I'll run the course you lay out for me if you'll just show me how. (Psalm 119:32 MSG)

Believers will take the time and make a quality decision to obey and follow God. This is regardless of the personal cost to the believer. The famous song tells us "I have decided to follow Jesus, no turning back, no turning back." (Author is anonymous) Being a follower of Jesus takes a strong, resolute decision and actions that correspond with a permanent decision. This means "no turning back."

Follow Jesus today. Follow His Word seriously and walk where He leads you.

Chapter Questions for Discussion or Study

1. FILL-IN: Psalm 35:19 NKJV - Let them not rejoice over me who are _____ my enemies; Nor let them wink with the eye who hate me without a _____.

2. Why did some people hate Jesus?

3. Where did the "haters" get the laws that they followed?

4. FILL-IN: Jesus the Messiah _____ followed God's Law. The Father's will became Jesus' _____. God's desires were written upon Jesus' _____.

5. FILL-IN: Psalm 40:7-8 NIV - Then I said, "Here I am, I have come - it is _____ about me in the scroll. I

_____ to do your will, my God; your law is within my _____."

6. Why should believers obey and do what God says and not add their own private interpretations?

John 15

Chapter 10

The Holy Spirit Will Come

Jesus told His disciples that the Holy Spirit would come.

> But I will send you the Advocate - the Spirit of truth. He will come to you from the Father and will testify all about me. And you must also testify about me because you have been with me from the beginning of my ministry. (John 15:26-27 NLT)

They would be able to tell people by clearly explaining all about Jesus. What He said, what He did and the hope we have in Him. This is important because followers of Jesus do not have to bring the good news in their own ability. They would receive the power they needed from the Holy Spirit.

Later, He told them to wait in Jerusalem until He sent God's power to them. He sent the Holy Spirit.

> I am going to send you what my Father has promised; but stay in the city until you have been clothed with power from on high." (Luke 24:29 NIV)

> "And now I will send the Holy Spirit, just as my Father promised. But stay here in the city until the Holy Spirit comes and fills you with power from heaven." (Luke 24:49 NLT)

God sent the Holy Spirit and the promise of the Father was fulfilled. It was exactly as Jesus had told the disciples.

> he gave them this command: "Do not leave Jerusalem, but wait for the gift my Father promised, which you have heard me speak about. (Acts 1:4b NIV)

> On the day of Pentecost all the believers were meeting together in one place. Suddenly, there was a sound from heaven like the roaring of a mighty windstorm, and it filled the house where they were sitting. Then, what looked like flames or tongues of fire appeared and settled on each of them. And everyone present was filled with the Holy Spirit and began speaking in other languages, as the Holy Spirit gave them this ability. (Acts 2:1-4 NLT)

Peter preached the gospel of Jesus Christ to the people who had gathered in the street after the Holy Spirit had come. Peter's words pierced their hearts. They were convinced of their need for God and 3000 listeners responded to God with faith. (Acts 2:14-41) The people heard the Word of God preached by Peter and saw their need for Jesus. Many became believers and were justified on that wonderful day in Jerusalem.

On another occasion, Peter and John brought the good news of His power and God healed the man.

> Peter and John went to the Temple one afternoon to participate in the three o'clock prayer service. As they approached the Temple, a man lame from birth was being carried in. Each day they put him beside the Temple gate, the one called the Beautiful Gate, so he could beg from the people going into the Temple. When he saw Peter and John about to enter, he asked them for some money. Peter and John looked at him intently, and Peter said, "Look at us!" The lame man looked at them eagerly, expecting some money. But Peter said, "I don't have any silver or gold for you. But I'll give you what I have. In the name of Jesus Christ the Nazarene, get up and walk!" Then Peter

> took the lame man by the right hand and helped him up. And as he did, the man's feet and ankles were instantly healed and strengthened. He jumped up, stood on his feet, and began to walk! Then, walking, leaping, and praising God, he went into the Temple with them. (Acts 3:1-8 NLT)

The disciples responded to this man's need and God healed him. The man immediately got to his feet. I have always liked the words that the man was "walking, leaping and praising God." (v.8) This can only be explained by God's miraculous healing flowing through the disciples.

The people in the crowd at the gate of the Temple were amazed.

> All the people saw him walking and praising God; and they recognized him as the very man who usually sat *begging* for coins at the Beautiful Gate of the temple, and they were filled with wonder and amazement *and* were mystified at what had happened to him. (Acts 3:9-10 AMP)

God, the Holy Spirit, moved in power and healed the crippled man. The man responded in faith to Peter's invitation by grasping his outstretched hand and walking!

Yet again, God brought a crowd of curious people and Peter began to preach the resurrection and healing power of Jesus Christ. (Acts 3:12-26)

> And while Peter and John were talking to the people, the priests and the captain [who was in charge of the temple area and] of the temple *guard* and the Sadducees came up to them, being extremely disturbed *and* thoroughly annoyed because they were teaching the people and proclaiming in [the case of] Jesus the resurrection of the dead. So they arrested them and put them in jail until the next day, because it was evening. But many of those who heard the message [of salvation] believed [in Jesus and accepted Him as the Christ]. And the number of the men came to be about 5,000. (Acts 4:1-4 AMP)

After the people received Christ, Peter and John were arrested for preaching the resurrection of Jesus. This demonstrated two things

- The religious leaders continued to really hate Jesus (see "They Hated Me" in the previous book chapter). The priests and Sadducees were totally offended when Peter and John healed the man and then preached the resurrection of Jesus. The disciples allowed the Holy Spirit to work through them and the power of God greatly offended the Temple priests.

> If the world hates you, remember that it hated me first. (John 15:18 NLT)

- This bitter and unfounded hatred of Jesus brought the arrest of Peter and John and they were thrown in jail. The leaders hated the Son of God because they had wrong thinking and demonstrated unbelief in the scriptures.

> Those who hate me without cause are more than the hairs of my head; Those who would destroy me are powerful, being my enemies wrongfully; I am forced to restore what I did not steal. (Psalm 69:4 AMP)

Peter and John preached Christ and God saved 5,000 people –their lives were changed! Thank God for His mercy and goodness and the wonderful salvation for those people who were saved!

This entire story of God giving the Holy Spirit (Acts 2) shows that the Fruit of the Spirit was fully evident in the disciples' lives (see book chapter 7 – Appointed To Bear Fruit). When the disciples ministered to the people, they showed love, joy, peace, patience, kindness, goodness, faithfulness, gentleness, and self-control. (Galatians 5:22-23a) The Fruit of the Spirit always comes when believers minister in the power of God the Holy Spirit.

A close examination of the crippled man's healing and their preaching shows that they worked together cooperatively with God the Holy Spirit. This is a perfect example of what God's expects of believers today. He gave the Holy Spirit to the Church and the Church is commissioned to carry the good news of Jesus to the entire world. Peter, John and the disciples started the process and the work has been continued down through the ages.

Today (now) the Church is responsible to work together with God. Working with God means we cooperate and act according to His wishes. We follow the leading of the Holy Spirit and tell people about the Lord Jesus.

Today, all believers need to make an active decision and follow God and work together with Him. Unbelievers ignore Him with an evil heart. Believers follow Him with a good heart full of righteousness that seeks God.

Remember what it says: "Today when you hear his voice, don't harden your hearts as Israel did when they rebelled." (Hebrews 3:15 NLT)

Remember, the Holy Spirit is present in the Church today – the Holy Spirit has come. Choose to actively obey Christ today and follow the Holy Spirit in all that you do.

Chapter Questions for Discussion or Study

1. FILL-IN: John 15:26-27 NLT - But I will send you the Advocate - the _____ _____ of truth. He will come to you from the _____ and will testify all about me. And you must also testify about me because you have been with me from the _____ of my ministry. (John 15:26-27 NLT)

2. FILL-IN: Luke 24:49 NLT - "And now I will send the _____, just as my Father promised. But stay _____ in the city until the Holy Spirit comes and _____ you with _____ from heaven." (Luke 24:49 NLT)

3. What happened on the day of Pentecost?

4. The crippled man was next to the gate of the Temple. What did Peter and John do? Why was this significant?

John 16
Preface

Before we head into the chapters of John 16, I want to bring you a

SPOILER ALERT!

John 16 ends with some excellent news! He finished telling the disciples to get ready for new things! Change is coming!

> These things I have spoken to you, that in Me you may have peace. In the world you will have tribulation; but be of good cheer, I have overcome the world. (John 16:33 NKJV)

> I have told you all this so that you may have peace in me. Here on earth you will have many trials and sorrows. But take heart, because I have overcome the world. (John 16:33 NLT)

> I have told you these things, so that in Me you may have [perfect] peace. In the world you have tribulation *and* distress *and* suffering, but be courageous [be confident, be undaunted, be filled with joy]; I have

overcome the world." [My conquest is accomplished, My victory abiding.] (John 16:33 AMP)

I've told you all this so that trusting me, you will be unshakable and assured, deeply at peace. In this godless world you will continue to experience difficulties. But take heart! I've conquered the world. (John 16:33 MSG)

This scripture changes an upcoming tough situation into a place where they will overcome. This is GREAT News!

Jesus was telling the disciples that trouble will definitely come, but cheer up – I have won and triumphed over it all! His words are good news for all believers in all generations. We can endure and triumph because Jesus won!

Go forward in Christ with this knowledge of God's victory.

John 16

Chapter 1

Where Will We Go?

John 16 begins with Jesus challenging His followers.

> I have told you these things so that you won't abandon your faith. For you will be expelled from the synagogues, and the time is coming when those who kill you will think they are doing a holy service for God. This is because they have never known the Father or me. (John 16:1-3 NLT)

I believe that this admonition and encouragement to the disciples was given because of the great opposition that Jesus had received throughout His ministry. Jesus knew that they would soon receive the opposition that He experienced. The book of Acts shows many examples where the disciples were opposed, harassed and persecuted.

Previously, the disciples showed their commitment to following Jesus. We read about this in John 6. Jesus challenged His followers with the level of commitment that they would have to make.

> And Jesus said to them, "I assure you *and* most solemnly say to you, unless you eat the flesh of the Son of Man and drink His blood [unless you believe in Me as Savior and believe in the saving power of My blood which will be shed for you], you do not have life in yourselves. (John 6:53 AMP)

This is a hard saying to accept, especially for a good, God-fearing Jew. They would say, "Really, are we eating flesh and drinking blood? Yuck! I won't do that!" But as believers, we know this is the basis of our commitment to Christ – His broken body and His shed blood. We celebrate His death, burial and resurrection when we take the symbols of Communion.

When all of this happened, many were offended and left Him. They abandoned the Messiah, the Son of God because He asked them to go deeper in their commitment to God. Jesus was calling them to have greater faith and devotion.

However, Peter and the other disciples of Jesus were different.

As a result of this many of His disciples abandoned Him, and no longer walked with Him. So Jesus said to the twelve [disciples], "You do not want to leave too, do you?" Simon Peter answered, "Lord, to whom shall we go? You [alone] have the words of eternal life [you are our only hope]. We have believed *and* confidently trusted, and [even more] we have come to know [by personal observation and experience] that You are the Holy One of God [the Christ, the Son of the living God]." (John 6:66-69 AMP)

Peter asked a GREAT question – "Lord, to whom shall we go?" Where else would they go to besides Jesus? They knew they had found the Messiah of God, the Christ who the Father had sent to His people. This as an essential question.

Every believer has been challenged to leave and forsake Christ. Circumstances, temptation, sin and frustration bring people to a place of – "should I stay or should I go?"

When I was challenged, God brought me to my senses when He asked, "Where are you going to go. You've found God through Christ - Jeffrey, don't quit now!" Thankfully, God kept me and I stayed with Him. He said He would not leave me or get rid of me. This is a simple idea, but at the same time, it is profound – God always protects me and wants me to stay close to Him!

This challenge to go deeper in their commitment to God is a central sticking point for many people. This commitment brings a deeper relationship with God. Many people see this as God wanting to control them, to make them into a preprogrammed, automatic robot that will blindly respond to God's wishes. Instead, we have a genuine relationship with God. It is a relationship of love. He loved us and we love Him. His love is why I follow and obey Him.

Believers must decide - do you want to hold the misconception that God is a heavenly despot who brings a heavy dose of divine control or is He a wonderful caring God who desires a loving relationship with you? The truth is that our loving God wants a meaningful, caring relationship with you.

We are still faced with the same choice today as in the past – do we choose belief or unbelief? Will we decide to follow Jesus?

Peter and the disciples chose to follow Jesus. He called them and they left their fishing businesses, tax collector jobs and other occupations. We saw in John 6 that they were challenged to decide to have a relationship with Christ. God called them to abide in Jesus Christ, the True Vine. They responded positively to Him and developed a relationship as they followed Him.

Jesus challenged them to break out of the day's religious lifestyle and follow Him. Many Jews felt that following rules and performing rituals were all there was to be Jewish. Following God had been reduced to a formula that denied the power of God and the necessity of a relationship with God.

The religious leaders had made their choice and created an entirely new religion based on or loosely connected to the true Law of Moses. Jesus called the leaders hypocrites for the minute management of people's lives and not living what the law tells the people to do.

> Woe to you, teachers of the law and Pharisees, you hypocrites! You give a tenth of your spices—mint, dill and cumin. But you have neglected the more important matters of the law—justice, mercy and faithfulness. You should have practiced the latter, without neglecting the former. (Matthew 23:23 NIV)

The religious leader did many things that were irrelevant to a relationship with God – the leaders practiced and lived unrelated side issues to the truth. Instead, Jesus told them to concentrate on justice, mercy and faithfulness.

Peter asked where else could they go to learn about God by following Him? The religious leaders had made up their minds to follow their religious traditions even though they were denying God. The disciples stated their intention to follow Him because He had the words of eternal life and He was the Messiah. (John 6:66-69)

Today, where will the believer go? Or better said, where will <u>you</u> go? We change the direction of our lives and set our feet on the right path when we follow Jesus. It starts with salvation and grows into a strong and thriving relationship with God. This relationship with God will be lived for a lifetime – it is permanent and eternal!

This is abiding in the True Vine. This is going to Jesus to connect with God. It is not a one-time religious experience or a keeping a set of rules. It is having a personal relationship with God through Jesus Christ.

Believers choose where they will go in their lives. Like Peter, believers make an eternal choice in their life about who they will serve. The religious leaders created their own man-made religion. Other people served false gods of wood and stone. Believers serve God through Jesus Christ.

Life is filled with a multitude of choices. Always choose to follow God through Jesus Christ.

Chapter Questions for Discussion or Study

1. FILL-IN: John 16:1 NLT – I have told you these things so that you won't _____ your faith.

2. Why did Jesus tell them not to abandon their faith?

3. Why did the offended people leave Jesus? What replacements for God do people go to when they reject God? What have you observed people seeking after?

4. Describe the challenges you experienced when you decided to accept Jesus and follow God?

5. What convinced you to accept that Jesus loves you?

6. Today, people need to receive and follow Jesus. What can believers do to bring people to Jesus?

John 16
Chapter 2
Hear Me Now

Jesus gave the disciples a warning.

> I have told you this, so that when their time comes you will remember that I warned you about them. I did not tell you this from the beginning because I was with you, but now I am going to him who sent me. (John 16:4-5a NIV)

They would receive persecution and opposition because of Him. Here, He is reminding them of this fact. Jesus is telling them to "get ready" because the hostility is coming.

This warning from Jesus directly answers the question, "why is this happening to me?" When we choose to follow God and live a life pleasing to Him, we will be persecuted simply because we love and follow Him. They hated Jesus, and they will hate the believer who follows Christ.

The believer must turn to God and not retaliate when persecution comes. Proverbs reminds us of the absolute necessity of hearing the Word of God. Listening to God and following Him are the only reactions we should have to persecution and opposition.

> My son, pay attention to what I say; turn your ear to my words. Do not let them out of your sight, keep them within your heart; for they are life to those who find them and health to one's whole body. (Proverbs 4:20-22 NIV)

Jesus turned to the Word of God and did not fight back.

> He did not retaliate when he was insulted nor threaten revenge when he suffered. He left his case in the hands of God, who always judges fairly. (1 Peter 2:23 NLT)

We see Jesus time and time again turning to God. He chose to hold God's Word as the final authority in His life.

When a believer chooses to hold God and His Word as the final authority, they choose the "God way." They are not limiting themselves. Instead, they are freeing themselves from following an ungodly lifestyle and the everyday, flesh-motivated way of thinking that is normal in society.

When I follow God's Word and the leading of God the Holy Spirit, I am doing the "right thing." I choose God's righteousness over serving my personal wishes or being "one of the crowd." Choosing God will make you different from people and pleasing to God.

We saw the importance of listening to and doing His Word. As we do this, we are also told to protect our hearts.

> Above all else, guard your heart, for everything you do flows from it. (Proverbs 4:23 NIV)

Above all else tells me that I have to do this first. It is important and demands immediate and ongoing attention.

Why is *guarding your heart* identified as being such an important issue? The heart is the origination point of everything that we do. The NLT tells us that the heart "determines the course of your life." A guarded heart means you choose the right course in life and that an unguarded heart brings many problems and ends in failure or destruction.

How do I follow this good advice and guard my heart? Proverbs 4:24-27 (NLT) lists these things.

- Do not engage in *perverse* talk.
  - This means do not participate in distorted or crooked speech.
  - It goes beyond discussing society's problems and tells the believer "do not talk about really stupid things" that distort serious matters and are definitely free from "dirty jokes."
- Stay away from *corrupt* speech.
  - Corrupt speech is devious talking.
  - One area to avoid is making jokes about sin.
  - The fool laughs about sin and "The stupid ridicule right and wrong" (Proverbs 14:9a MSG)
  - It is common practice for society to dismiss sin as unimportant or permissible and just another aspect of a chosen lifestyle.
  - When people say "to each his own," they say that everyone can determine right and wrong. People create and follow their moral laws. By this reckoning, there are no absolutes. Without God's moral authority, people will "do their own thing" - make self-

determined choices that deny God. Believers choose to follow God and His absolute authority.
- When confronted with sin, believers should run!
- Keep your eyes *looking straight ahead*.
  - This is best accomplished by looking at God and His Word. Do not look at or engage in sinful side issues.

Do not choose to become involved with sin. Believers should "shun and run!"

- Do not wander into known sin. Casual acceptance of sin can be avoided by being aware of your actions and the circumstances around you.
- Unintentional sin is still sin. When we sin, we ignore God and allow our flesh to make decisions about our life.
  - Rebelling against God is like the sin of witchcraft (1 Samuel 15:23) – creating a man-made religion that denies God.
- If you sin and "lose your way," get back to God's pathway – follow what God tells believers in His Word and listen for the still small voice of the Holy Spirit leading you.

When believers follow God, they take His direction in their lives. When changes and challenges come, believers don't get "off track" like a train derailing. They follow God and fulfill their destiny.

> Turn not to the right hand nor the left: remove thy foot from evil. (Proverbs 4:27 KJV)

Believers stay on God's set course. They follow the "track" that He has laid out before them.

The NLT uses the word *sidetracked* to describe turning to the right or left.

Isn't it funny how we choose the things that are just OK and not choose the excellent, superior things that are available? Bad choices bring bad outcomes. "God choices" bring righteous outcomes.

God always brings excellent and superior things – they are always better than the "just OK." God wants us to choose Him and bring Him honor with our choices.

> Today I have given you the choice between life and death, between blessings and curses. Now I call on heaven and earth to witness the choice you make. Oh, that you would choose

life, so that you and your descendants might live! (Deuteronomy 30:19 NLT)

In Deuteronomy 30:20 (MSG), we choose to follow and obey God. We embrace Him because we know He will bring us to walk in the Truth of Jesus Christ.

> And love GOD, your God, listening obediently to him, firmly embracing him. Oh yes, he is life itself, a long life settled on the soil that GOD, your God, promised to give your ancestors, Abraham, Isaac, and Jacob. (Deuteronomy 30:20 MSG)

The Jews were given the land that He promised Abraham simply because God loved them. But they had to exercise obedience. Believers are given eternal life that starts the day we follow God through Jesus Christ. We obey the Gospel of Jesus Christ and begin our life with Him.

In closing, we choose to follow God's Word in the Bible. This is the righteous choice that honors God and brings Him glory. We recognize that He is God and choose to follow Him permanently.

Chapter Questions for Discussion or Study

1. What happens when a believer chooses to hold God and His Word as the final authority in their life?

2. FILL-IN: When I follow God's Word and the leading of God the Holy _____, I am doing the "right thing." I am choosing God's _____ over serving my personal _____ or being "one of the crowd."

3. What is "perverse talk?" Why should believers avoid it?

4. What is "corrupt speech?" Why should believers stay away from it?

5. What is "looking straight ahead?" Why should believers do this?

6. Believers should not become involved with things that are sin. What should they do when they are tempted or actually sin?

7. If a believer sins, what should they do to get back to God's pathway for their life?

8. Why did God give the land that He promised?

John 16
Chapter 3
It's Time For Me To Go

A lot of popular songs contain lyrics about being apart and missing someone. Judy Collins (in the 1960s) performed a song called *Someday Soon*. It told the story of a young woman who longed to see her boyfriend while he competed in the rodeo. He lived on the road as he traveled from town to town (rodeo to rodeo). He would spend days away while he "rides the rodeo." Despite the heartache and challenges she experienced, she sang that "someday soon, going with him, someday soon." She was sad but soon would be glad.

Jesus spoke to His disciples and told them that He was leaving.

> none of you asks Me, 'Where are You going?' But because I have said these things to you, sorrow has filled your heart. Nevertheless I tell you the truth. It is to your advantage that I go away (John 16:5b-7 NKJV)

The main difference in these stories is that Jesus would be reunited with His disciples very soon – only a few days after He spoke these words! Jesus told them that even though "sorrow has filled their heart(s)," it is best that I go away. They did not know the events that would happen later that evening and for the rest of the Passover weekend. Jesus knew what would happen and understood that He needed to encourage His followers.

Jesus would tell them that hope was definitely in order and that they should have hope in Him. Jesus declared victory before He suffered, died and was raised from the dead.

> These things I have spoken to you, that in Me you may have peace. In the world you will have tribulation; but be of good cheer, I have overcome the world. (John 16:33 NKJV)

> I have told you all this so that you may have peace in me. Here on earth you will have many trials and sorrows. But take heart, because I have overcome the world. (John 16:33 NLT)

Jesus knew the beginning and He knew the end. He told them to "hang in there" because even though there would be significant problems, they should hold on. After all, He had overcome. Jesus would say, "I am the victor!"

But the immediate problem for the disciples was "where is Jesus going and what are we going to do?" They were grieving the terrible news they had received. I would add, "Jesus, why are You leaving?"

Jesus answered these questions with these words -

- He was leaving them to return to the Father. (v.5)
- He had to leave for the Holy Spirit to come to them. (v.7)

He would never leave the disciples or get rid of them, so they had the assurance of God that Jesus would always be with them.

Even though the disciples knew that opposition was coming, I am sure that they wondered how they would handle the daily challenges without Jesus. He had always defended them and stopped those who opposed God. How could they go on? "Jesus is leaving. God help us!"

Moses had made it very clear. As good Jewish men, they would have known the scripture that told the story of Joshua and the story of conquering the Promised Land.

> Be strong and courageous. Do not be afraid or terrified because of them, for the LORD your God goes with you; he will never leave you nor forsake you. (Deuteronomy 31:6 NIV)

The disciples did not realize that God would always be there for them. Jesus was leaving, but the Holy Spirit was coming at the same time!

Today we can stand back from this situation and realize that conquering the Promised Land and bringing Jesus to the people of the world were similar challenges. They were not alone, but God would be helping them. "Nobody can oppose me and win - God is on my side!"

> If God is for us, who can ever be against us? (Romans 8:31b NLT)

We can carry out His will and successfully follow His perfect leading.

For the disciples, the Holy Spirit would lead them, guide them and give them power from God. With the Holy Spirit, they were fully and properly equipped – they had everything that they needed. For us, believers bring the good news to people, we pray with and for people and we always help people.

> For I can do everything through Christ, who gives me strength. (Philippians 4:13 NLT)
>
> I can do all things [which He has called me to do] through Him who strengthens *and* empowers me [to fulfill His purpose - I am self-sufficient in Christ's sufficiency; I am ready for anything and equal to anything through Him who infuses me with inner strength and confident peace (Philippians 4:13 AMP)

This is a wonderful promise from God – He assures us of His strength and of His sufficiency in our lives. He pours His power into us and gives us the ability to work for Him successfully. When Jesus told them <u>why</u> He was going away, He told them He was going to the Father. In this, He would send the Holy Spirit.

> But in fact, it is best for you that I go away, because if I don't, the Advocate won't come. If I do go away, then I will send him to you. (John 16:7 NLT)

God, the Holy Spirit, gives power to us. We accomplish the things that we believe. Jesus told us to have faith in God, who gives us the power of the Holy Spirit when we have faith in Him.

A light bulb needs the power of electricity to illuminate and bring light to the darkness. Jesus does not send believers out ill-equipped, but they have everything they need because He sent the Holy Spirit. A believer needs the power of the Holy Spirit to fully and correctly serve God. Jesus knew the need for this power from God and the Holy Spirit came upon Him when John baptized Him in water.

> Then John testified, "I saw the Holy Spirit descending like a dove from heaven and resting upon him. I didn't know he was the one, but when God sent me to baptize with water, he told me, 'The one on whom you see the Spirit descend and rest is the one who will baptize with the Holy Spirit.' I saw this happen to Jesus, so I testify that he is the Chosen One of God." (John 1:32-34 NLT)

After the resurrection and His return to God, Jesus sent the Holy Spirit to the believers in Jerusalem. They were obeying Jesus by waiting until the Holy Spirit arrived. (Luke 24:49) All of the miraculous events in Acts depended upon the work of the Holy Spirit. If the disciples did not have the Holy Spirit, they would act on their own authority without God's power. They would be like a light bulb with no electricity.

Peter preached the power-filled message in Acts 2 because the Holy Spirit worked through Him. Peter cooperated with God, and God brought many people to Christ. Peter and John (Acts 3) brought God's healing to the crippled man because of the power of the Holy Spirit was in them.

Today we can bring God's good news to the people of our society because of the power of the Holy Spirit. When people tell others about God <u>without</u> the Holy Spirit, they are using their own power. It is simply another religion. When believers work closely with the Holy Spirit and preach the Word of God, it is God-centered and power-filled. This is the good news that will bring people to salvation in Christ, bring healing to them and give them God's power to help others. This is the Gospel in action – God sending His good news to people one at a time!

After Jesus went to the Father, He sent the Holy Spirit. Every time He empowered another believer, it was one more person that could carry the Gospel and minister to people instead of Jesus being on earth. On the morning of the day of Pentecost (Acts 2), about 120 people were praying and worshipping God. At the end of the day, there were about 3,000 more righteous people full of the Holy Spirit. Immediately, Jesus the Messiah was now "spread out" to be used by God. There was still Jesus and now, about 3,120 believers full of God's power.

From this point forward, newly saved people were being added daily to the Body of Christ. (Acts 2:47) The new people were like Jesus being on earth and doing God's work. Now, more believers were ready to go and do greater works for God. (John 14:12) How many salivation, healings and other miracles did the disciples do that went unrecorded?

Jesus on earth before the resurrection could be considered a "small footprint" of God's wonderful presence. He was active and helped people, but He was one man at one place at one time. God's plan was always to send the Holy Spirit to empower believers to carry the Gospel to the world.

After the Holy Spirit was poured out, there was a greater effect of the presence of God. This greater effect is shown in a local community with one Bible-believing church and another community with five Bible-believing churches working together to bring the Gospel to people. More active churches mean more community involvement and influence through the proclamation of Jesus Christ.

Today, the Gospel is being effectively proclaimed because Jesus went to be with the

Father and sent His Holy Spirit to the people of the Church. As believers, we humbly take His Word and His power and go to everyone everywhere.

Missions to the unsaved involve your neighborhood as well as West Africa, South America and Asia. Today, believers tell the stories of Jesus, declare His salvation to people, heal the sick, raise the dead and help people. Let us believe God, receive and obey the Holy Spirit and let us go to the people of the world in His name.

Chapter Questions for Discussion or Study

1. Jesus was crucified on the cross. What happened before He returned to the earth and His disciples?

2. FILL-IN John 16:33 NLT: I have told you all this so that you may have _____ in me. Here on earth you will have many _____. But take heart, because I have _____ the world.

3. FILL-IN Deuteronomy 16:33 NIV - Be strong and courageous. Do not be _____ because of them, for the LORD your God goes with you; he

will never _____ you nor _____ you.

4. Write 3 things that the Holy Spirit did for the disciples?

5. Why can believers do all things through Christ? (Philippians 4:13)

6. Why do believers need the Holy Spirit like a light bulb needs electricity?

7. Peter effectively preached to the crowd in Acts 2. How did he do this?

8. It is better to have Jesus on the earth or have many believers full of God the Holy Spirit?

9. What is meant by a "small footprint of God's wonderful presence?"

John 16
Chapter 4
Sin, Righteousness And Judgement

When writing this chapter, I chose the title *Sin, Righteous And Judgement*. This is a solid title, but it might be a bit overwhelming. I believe that understanding this helps us to enter into His rest and the presence of God.

These strong words are crucial to understanding God and living our lives for Him.

> And when he comes, he will convict the world of its sin, and of God's righteousness, and of the coming judgment. The world's sin is that it refuses to believe in me. Righteousness is available because I go to the Father, and you will see me no more. Judgment will come because the ruler of this world has already been judged. (John 16:8-11 NLT)
>
> When he comes, he'll expose the error of the godless world's view of sin, righteousness, and judgment: He'll show

> them that their refusal to believe in me is their basic sin; that righteousness comes from above, where I am with the Father, out of their sight and control; that judgment takes place as the ruler of this godless world is brought to trial and convicted. (John 16:8-11 MSG)

Sin can best be described as breaking God's Law, missing the mark and violating His holy standards. Every human has sinned, and all sin is ultimately against God.

> for all have sinned and fall short of the glory of God, (Romans 3:23 NIV)

> Against you, and you alone, have I sinned; I have done what is evil in your sight. You will be proved right in what you say, and your judgment against me is just. (Psalm 51:4 NLT)

We break the law of God when we hurt someone with our selfishness. However, when we sin, the sin is done against God. Sin is like telling God, "I will not live according to what You want and I will make all of my own rules and decisions!" We are letting God know that we will act without His guidance.

> If we say that we have no sin, we deceive ourselves, and the truth is not in us. (1 John 1:8 NKJV)

Everyone has sinned and everyone needs to come clean before God.

The good news is that we can be released from sin. Jesus paid for our sin when He died on the cross and was resurrected by God. Jesus bought us freedom from sin and gave us the righteousness of God. Believers now have right standing with God.

He will convince and convict the people of this world that *righteousness* is God's standard. People must receive from God to be able to receive righteousness from him.
Righteousness is God's character and His way of doing things. His standard is perfection - all of the time. God has integrity. He is pure and always thinks and acts right. God is not stupid, confused and He does not make mistakes. He always has a plan and it is perfect.

Believers need the high standards of God, which Jesus Christ lived when He was on the earth. Humans cannot keep God's standards in their own power but in the power of the Holy Spirit.

> Do you not know that when you *continually* offer yourselves to someone to do his will, you are the slaves of the one whom you obey, either [slaves] of sin, which leads to death, or of obedience, which leads to

righteousness (right standing with God)? (Romans 6:16 AMP)

Believers must continually be in communication with God and live His righteousness. This is His high standard, and it is the power of the Holy Spirit that helps us. We have been recreated from death to life in this new life of God's righteousness in our lives.

Judgment is simple. Judgment is condemnation because of guilt. In a courtroom, judgment occurs when a person has been found or judged guilty. The guilty person is sentenced for their crime. In God's world, people are condemned to eternal death for refusing to accept God's perfect gift – His Son Jesus.

Believers have been mercifully forgiven because of Jesus. This is clearly shown in John 3.

> For God so loved the world, that he gave his only begotten Son, that whosoever believeth in him should not perish, but have everlasting life. For God sent not his Son into the world to condemn the world; but that the world through him might be saved. He that believeth on him is not condemned: but he that believeth not is condemned

already, because he hath not believed in the name of the only begotten Son of God. (John 3:16-18 KJV)

For God so [greatly] loved *and* dearly prized the world, that He [even] gave His [One and] only begotten Son, so that whoever believes *and* trusts in Him [as Savior] shall not perish, but have eternal life. For God did not send the Son into the world to judge *and* condemn the world [that is, to initiate the final judgment of the world], but that the world might be saved through Him. Whoever believes *and* has decided to trust in Him [as personal Savior and Lord] is not judged [for this one, there is no judgment, no rejection, no condemnation]; but the one who does not believe [and has decided to reject Him as personal Savior and Lord] is judged already [that one has been convicted and sentenced], because he has not believed *and* trusted in the name of the [One and] only begotten Son of God [the One who is truly unique, the only One of His kind, the One who alone can save him]. (John 3:16-18 AMP)

God sent Jesus on a mission. He was to bring forgiveness to people, not condemnation for their sin. Judgment was put in place for the devil and his demons. They have been condemned for rebellion toward God. People receive eternal condemnation and death when they do not acknowledge and receive Jesus as their Lord and Savior. They refuse eternal life and choose the eternal "default" by doing nothing which results in eternal separation from God and being condemned to hell forever.

The tragedy and fundamental problem is that God chooses eternal life for everyone. Instead of receiving it and embracing Him, people do not decide to follow Christ and are lost forever.

This scripture sums it up nicely.

> Today I have given you the choice between life and death, between blessings and curses. Now I call on heaven and earth to witness the choice you make. Oh, that you would choose life, so that you and your descendants might live! (Deuteronomy 30:19 NLT)

The context of this scripture is the people's need to obey the Law God gave through Moses. The more significant application is "will <u>you</u> receive Christ and obey God?"

When God works to convince the world of their need for Him, He is dealing with many people who do not believe in God. Many of these people have chosen to follow their own beliefs about life. This is why God must convince people to leave their old life and receive God's new life from Him. To *convince* is to cause someone to believe firmly in His existence and ability to save them. Jesus came to do this on earth as He taught the Truth and continues to do this today through the Holy Spirit.

The religious leaders accused Jesus of being a blasphemer, someone who spoke profanity about God. The religious leaders condemned Him because He claimed He to have a special relationship with God and they took His claim as profanity. For this, He was judged guilty.

It was a miscarriage of justice that Jesus was accused and an even greater injustice that He was convicted, condemned and crucified.

> He was oppressed and treated harshly, yet he never said a word. He was led like a lamb to the slaughter. And as a sheep is silent before the shearers, he did not open his mouth. (Isaiah 53:7 NLT)

He willingly took the pain, suffering and punishment for everyone because He loves us. He loves everyone, not just the good people or the religious people.

> Greater love has no one than this: to lay down one's life for one's friends. (John 15:13 NIV)

Jesus was <u>not</u> a blasphemer. He was (and is) the Son of God and the Messiah, sent by God to redeem all people. He was hated and dismissed by people despite who He was.

> He was despised and rejected by men, A Man of sorrows *and* pain and acquainted with grief; And like One from whom men hide their faces He was despised, and we did not appreciate His worth *or* esteem Him. (Isaiah 53:3 AMP)

It seems so odd that people would hate and reject Jesus, the Son of God. He was treated as a lowly ordinary person and put to death as a criminal. I have to remember that <u>I</u> hated and rejected Jesus before I was saved; this is how most people feel about God today. Many people are religious with their mouths but evil in their hearts and how they reject God.

This is where sin comes in. People miss the mark because they reject God and do not realize that man cannot approach God without Jesus. The religious leaders in Jesus' day were in sin because they rejected Him. It is the same thing with people rejecting Jesus today. They might go to church or believe in God but say, "I don't want <u>anyone</u> controlling my life!" This includes almighty God wanting to bring His love to all people everywhere.

How is the response of believers different? Believers tell God "I love You because You first loved me." Jesus invited us to come to Him and He would give us rest and peace in God. We will experience a new life because we receive salvation from God through Jesus.

Receive His mission of helping people today. Come to Jesus and receive the freedom of salvation. This is possible because He has forgiven people of their *sin*, provided His *righteousness* from God and the devil has been *judged*. Jesus has triumphed over the devil, evil, and sin by His resurrection. We receive His goodness and carry it to other people.

Chapter Questions for Discussion or Study

1. What is the best description for *sin*?

2. What is *righteousness*?

3. What is *judgement*?

4. FILL-IN John 3:16-18 KJV: For God so _____ the world, that he gave his only begotten Son, that whosoever _____ in

him should not perish, but have everlasting life. For God sent not his Son into the world to _____ the world; but that the world through him might be _____. He that believeth on him is not _____: but he that believeth not is _____ already, because he hath not believed in the name of the only begotten Son of God.

5. What was the nature of the mission that God sent Jesus to accomplish?

6. In Deuteronomy 30:19 NLT, what should believers choose?

7. Why did the religious leaders consider Jesus a blasphemer?

John 16

Chapter 5

He Will Guide Us In All Truth

Jesus told the disciples that God would be with them. But, Jesus was going away. How could God be with them if Jesus left them? Jesus had been their point of contact with God, but now He was leaving.

> I still have many things to say to you, but you cannot bear *them* now. However, when He, the Spirit of truth, has come, He will guide you into all truth; for He will not speak on His own *authority,* but whatever He hears He will speak; and He will tell you things to come. He will glorify Me, for He will take of what is Mine and declare *it* to you. All things that the Father has are Mine. Therefore I said that He will take of Mine and declare *it* to you. (John 16:12-15 NKJV)

> I still have many things to tell you, but you can't handle them now. But when the Friend comes, the Spirit of the Truth, he will take you by the hand and guide you into all the truth there is. He won't draw attention to himself, but will make sense out of what is about to happen and, indeed, out of all that I have done and said. He will honor me; he will take from me and deliver it to you. Everything the Father has is also mine. That is why I've said, He takes from me and delivers to you. (John 16:12-15 MSG)

Jesus told them that God the Holy Spirit would come and guide them "into all truth." He would explain the things that Jesus told them as well as the Law and the Prophets. This means He would help people to discover, receive and know God. This was the reason He came to earth – to bring people to God. People would be free and unhindered in God because they would know the truth. (John 8:32)

Jesus told the disciples that they could not bear or endure what He needed to say to them. However, the situation would change <u>after</u> the resurrection when they would be born again and filled with the Holy Spirit. They would become spiritually alive and full of the power of God. Jesus would send the disciples and the believers who would come later to carry the

Gospel to the entire world. When the Father sent the Holy Spirit, things became different. His followers would now receive power from the Holy Spirit.

The Holy Spirit would use His power to guide us to grow in our relationship with Jesus. As we know Jesus more and more, we grow in our knowledge of the Truth. This is much more than just knowing <u>about</u> the Truth, it is personally knowing Him, the Truth of God. Knowing Jesus equips us to serve Him effectively as we help people.

The emphasis in this text is on the coming of the Holy Spirit. He would send the Holy Spirit, who would "take you by the hand and guide you into all the truth there is." This is a wonderful promise from Jesus that applies to us today as much as it applied to the disciples that evening.

As the Holy Spirit guides us into all truth, we are assured that He will personally be with us. I can be confident that Truth is what I am getting.

Many religions emphasize gaining enlightenment or searching for God. The Bible teaches that if we seek the true God with all of our hearts, we will find Him.

> Then [with a deep longing] you will seek Me *and* require Me [as a vital necessity] and [you will] find Me when you search for Me with all your heart. I will be found by you, says the LORD, (Jeremiah 29:13-14a AMP)

When someone finally gets to their own end and calls out to God, they will find Him and He will help them. Religion seeks to know about God, but Jesus came to reveal God to us personally. This is a promise and God always keeps His promises.

The Holy Spirit will not speak of Himself. When the Holy Spirit came in Acts 2, Peter went out and preached to the assembled crowd in the street. He told them about Jesus.

> Therefore let all Israel be assured of this: God has made this Jesus, whom you crucified, both Lord and Messiah. (Acts 2:36 NIV)

The Holy Spirit inspired Peter to talk about Jesus. Peter told the crowd what Jesus did and why people needed to receive Him as Lord and Savior. The people responded and the results were fantastic! This speaks of the power of the Holy Spirit and His ministry to people through believers.

> When the people heard this, they were cut to the heart and said to Peter and the other apostles, "Brothers, what shall we do?" Peter replied, "Repent and be baptized, every one of you, in the name of Jesus Christ for the forgiveness of your sins. And you will receive the gift of the Holy Spirit. The promise is for you and your children and for all who are far off—for all whom the Lord our God will call." With many other words he warned them; and he pleaded with them, "Save yourselves from this corrupt generation." Those who accepted his message were baptized, and about three thousand were added to their number that day. (Acts 2:37-41)

Peter cooperated with the Holy Spirit. As he worked with God, Peter preached to the people, who were "cut to the heart." Their ability to respond YES to God was definitely present and they accepted Peter's message. This is the same Holy Spirit today – He leads people to Jesus and challenges them to receive Jesus and make Him their Lord and Savior.

The Holy Spirit speaks what He hears from God. This is important to understand. The Holy Spirit speaks about Jesus because He is the only way to reach God. Religion, philosophy and selfless service to other people do not get you to God. The Holy Spirit convinces us that Jesus is the way. The Holy Spirit leads us right to Jesus and helps us to receive and follow Him.

The Holy Spirit will speak of the Father and remind us of what Jesus told us.

> On that day you will ask in My name, and I am not saying to you that I will request of the Father on your behalf; (John 16:26 NKJV)

Believers ask the Father for many different things – "visit my family who needs you and draw them to You" or "Father, I need _____ ...", etc. After a believer prays to the Father, it is time to thank Him. Jesus said we would have what we pray for.

> Jesus replied, "Have faith in God [constantly]. I assure you *and* most solemnly say to you, whoever says to this mountain, 'Be lifted up and thrown into the sea!' and does not doubt in his heart [in God's unlimited power], but believes that what he says is going to take place, it will be done for him [in accordance with God's will]. For this reason I am telling you, whatever things you ask for in prayer [in accordance with God's will], believe [with confident trust] that you have received them, and

they will be *given* to you. (Mark 11:22-24 AMP)

It is essential to ask for the things that are consistent with His Word and His revealed will. I will not ask for something that I know is not His will. My Father knows best and I am ready to receive His wishes.

God helps His children according to His timetable. God is always on time and never late. Regardless of the expectations of time that I put on Him ("Hurry up Lord. You know I am impatient!"), my heavenly Father will answer my prayers. This is what the Bible teaches.

The Holy Spirit will tell us of things to come. He will reveal things from God that He wants us to know. I have learned to rely on the Holy Spirit to guide me in big and small things. I want to follow God and be in the right place at the right time and know what matters to God. I am thankful for the guidance of the Holy Spirit.

We will hear and obey what the Holy Spirit says to us. We know from the prophet Samuel the importance of obeying God.

> But Samuel replied, "What is more pleasing to the LORD: your burnt offerings and sacrifices or your obedience to his voice? Listen!

> Obedience is better than sacrifice, and submission is better than offering the fat of rams. (1 Samuel 15:22 NLT)

> He wants you to listen to him and do what He tells you! Plain listening is the thing, not staging a lavish religious production. Not doing what GOD tells you is far worse than fooling around in the occult. (1 Samuel 15:22 MSG)

Friends work together. Abraham and Noah both worked closely with God. The believers' friendship with God is through our Lord and Savior, Jesus Christ. We are friends with God.

I choose to obey God because I love Him. It's not me acting like a robot but is a voluntary thing. God loved me first and I chose to follow Him.

Jesus told them He had to leave and they wouldn't see Him. Then He would come back.

> "In a little while, you won't see me anymore. But a little while after that, you will see me again." Some of the disciples asked each other, "What does he mean when he says, 'In a little while you won't see me, but then you will see me,' and 'I am going to the Father'? And what does he mean by 'a little while'?

We don't understand." (John 16:16-18 NLT)

The disciples were frustrated because they couldn't fully comprehend what He told them. They had many questions. He would leave them when He was arrested and crucified and return to them after the resurrection. The disciples would eventually understand.

I believe they lost all hope when they saw Him die on the cross. They had been with Jesus every day for about 3½ years. All of the events with the crucifixion and resurrection were a shock. There were not ordinary, everyday experiences.

The importance of Jesus going away is found in what would happen. His departure was because of the brutal crucifixion. He suffered and died. It was God's will that He die. This was not a chance encounter street murder, but it was God's plan to sacrifice the sinless Son of God for all of our sins. This is why it was critical for Jesus to go away and then return – His death and resurrection brought new life to His Body, the Church.

In closing, it is only through the life-changing resurrection of Jesus that we can come to God and know Him.

Chapter Questions for Discussion or Study

1. FILL-IN: _____ told them that God the _____ _____ would guide them into all truth.

2. FILL-IN: After the resurrection the disciples were _____ again and filled with the _____ _____.

3. How were the followers of Jesus changed after they were filled with the Holy Spirit?

4. Why should believers be thankful that they are filled with the Holy Spirit?

5. How has the Holy Spirit changed your life as a believer?

6. Why is it important to pray and ask God according to His will for your life?

7. What did the prophet Samuel say that obedience to God is better than?

John 16
Chapter 6
No One Can Rob You Of That Joy

Jesus clarified to the disciples that His crucifixion would bring grief and sadness far beyond "having a bad day."

> I tell you the truth, you will weep and mourn over what is going to happen to me, but the world will rejoice. You will grieve, but your grief will suddenly turn to wonderful joy. It will be like a woman suffering the pains of labor. When her child is born, her anguish gives way to joy because she has brought a new baby into the world. So you have sorrow now, but I will see you again; then you will rejoice, and no one can rob you of that joy. (John 16:20-22 NLT)

Jesus said that they would not be able to deal with the stress and burden that would soon occur. His death and resurrection would go way beyond human comprehension. Jesus told the disciples that evening that their joy could not be stolen! All of the grief, the sadness, the violence and the tragedy would not steal their joy. God would protect His children so their joy would remain intact.

Jesus compared the grief they would suffer to the physical pain that a woman experiences in childbirth. But after the pain and the baby being born, there is GREAT JOY! The pain was very real, but it is overshadowed by the birth of a wonderful new child. Whether it is the first child or the tenth, it is a matter of joy for the family.

And no one can rob you of that joy that God gave you this joy through the Holy Spirit. A song by Shirley Caesar brings this idea to light.

> This joy that I have the world didn't give to me,
>
> The world didn't give it and the world can't take it away.
>
> Who gave it to you? Jesus Jesus Jesus!
>
> (Shirley Caesar, Public Domain)

After Jesus was crucified, His dead body was placed in a tomb on Friday. On the Sunday morning after the sabbath, Mary Magdalene went to the tomb. She discovered that the stone covering the entryway into the tomb had been rolled away. She was upset, and the Lord appeared. She knew it was Jesus. (Summary of John 20:1-18)

Her surprise at finding Jesus alive was accompanied by joy. She went back to the disciples and told them that she had seen the Lord.

Later, Thomas (who is called "doubting Thomas") wanted physical evidence to prove Jesus was alive.

> One of the twelve disciples, Thomas (nicknamed the Twin), was not with the others when Jesus came. They told him, "We have seen the Lord!" But he replied, "I won't believe it unless I see the nail wounds in his hands, put my fingers into them, and place my hand into the wound in his side." Eight days later the disciples were together again, and this time Thomas was with them. The doors were locked; but suddenly, as before, Jesus was standing among them. "Peace be with you," he said. Then he said to Thomas, "Put your finger here, and look at my hands. Put your hand into the wound in my side. Don't be faithless any longer. Believe!" "My Lord and my God!" Thomas exclaimed. (John 20:24-28 NLT)

Thomas refused to believe and demanded evidence to prove His resurrection from the dead. Jesus came to Thomas and the disciples and Thomas exclaimed, "My Lord and my God!" Thomas had great joy. Suddenly he became "believing Thomas."

Jesus said He would give us a full dose of God's joy when we obey Him and receive His love.

> I have told you this so that my joy may be in you and that your joy may be complete. (John 15:11 NIV)

People today experience that same joy when they have an encounter with Jesus. This experience changes people's lives for a lifetime.

The Holy Spirit permanently lives within us. He produces God's joy because of His presence in our lives. He gladly radiates joy which fills us and spills over to those around us. This is the fruit of the Spirit. (Galatians 5:22) Apple trees produce apples and the Holy Spirit produces in us the different qualities that make up the character of God.

> But the fruit of the Spirit is love, joy, peace, forbearance, kindness, goodness, faithfulness, gentleness and self-control. Against such things there is no law. (Galatians 5:22-23 NIV)

> But the Holy Spirit produces this kind of fruit in our lives: love, joy, peace, patience, kindness, goodness, faithfulness, gentleness, and self-control. There is no law against these things! (Galatians 5:22-23 NLT)

Joy is one of the fruits of the Spirit. God the Holy Spirit gives these fruits, and one of these fruits is His joy in us.

We are strong in the Lord because we have His joy.

> Don't be dejected and sad, for the joy of the LORD is your strength! (Nehemiah 8:10b)

Nehemiah and Ezra were faced with some tough situations that brought great challenges to them. Despite these challenges, they kept themselves firmly planted in God's joy. Today, believers must allow God's joy to "bubble up and flow out" from within you. We use it to stay strong and to serve God. We give God's joy to others.

Believers pray to God using the authority of the name of Jesus. It's not a code word or some kind of magic. Instead it is us talking to God because we <u>can</u> talk to Him. Jesus brings us to the Father and we can now ask Him for what we need. We can talk to Him when we are happy and when we are sad.

> So you have sorrow now, but I will see you again; then you will rejoice, and no one can rob you of that joy. At that time you won't need to ask me for anything. I tell you the truth, you will ask the Father directly, and he will grant your request because you use my name. You haven't done this before. Ask, using my name, and you will receive, and you will have abundant joy. (John 16:22-24 NLT)

They rejoiced when the disciples saw Jesus after He rose from the dead. Their joy was flowing over the crowd as they preached and shared Jesus on the day of Pentecost. The 3,000 people who accepted Jesus that day could see that the disciples were different. They were full of the joy of the Lord!

In closing, believers who yield to God and the work of His Holy Spirit, receive and give joy to others. This is the mission of the Church. It consists of the Church doing the work of the Lord on this earth.

GO JESUS!!!

Chapter Questions for Discussion or Study

1. FILL-IN: I tell you the truth, you will weep and _____ over what is going to happen to me, but the world will _____.

2. FILL-IN: All of the grief, the sadness, the violence and the tragedy would not steal their _____.

3. Her surprise at finding Jesus alive was accompanied by joy. She went back to the disciples and told them that she had seen the Lord. How would you have reacted if you had been in her place?

4. Nehemiah and Ezra faced some tough situations that brought a great challenge to them. Despite these challenges, they kept themselves firmly planted in God's joy. Describe situations where you lost your joy and where you held onto your joy in God.

5. What did the disciples do after Jesus rose from the dead?

John 16
Chapter 7
Now It's All Clear

Jesus talked to His disciples and the people using parables – stories used to teach a principle or help make a point. One day the disciples asked Jesus, "why?"

> Then the disciples came to Him and asked, "Why do You speak to the crowds in parables?" Jesus replied to them, "To you it has been granted to know the mysteries of the kingdom of heaven, but to them it has not been granted. For whoever has [spiritual wisdom because he is receptive to God's word], to him *more* will be given, and he will be richly *and* abundantly supplied; but whoever does not have [spiritual wisdom because he has devalued God's word], even what he has will be taken away from him. (Matthew 13:10-12 AMP)

The parables are rich when they are read. These stories help make the idea that is being taught come alive. The disciples were challenged when they tried to understand them.

> I have spoken of these matters in figures of speech, but soon I will stop speaking figuratively and will tell you plainly all about the Father. (John 16:25 NLT)

As believers study the parables, they become understandable and their meaning becomes apparent. This is because the Holy Spirit makes the parables "alive." He transforms words on a page into ideas and concepts that become a "living word" to us. The parables become personal to each of us because God the Holy Spirit reveals their meaning to us. We suddenly begin to better understand His words because the Holy Spirit teaches us the power-filled Truth of His Word.

> For the word of God is living and active *and* full of power [making it operative, energizing, and effective]. It is sharper than any two-edged sword, (Hebrews 4:12a AMP)

Jesus revealed the new Truth to His disciples. They would now be talking directly to the

Father. No longer would they ask Jesus to speak to the Father for them.

> In that day you will ask in My name, and I do not say to you that I shall pray the Father for you; for the Father Himself loves you, because you have loved Me, and have believed that I came forth from God. (John 16:26-27 NKJV)

Jesus said that we now ask and speak to the Father. I can talk to the Father anywhere, anytime and for any reason. The Father loves me and wants to talk to me. This is because I love Jesus and have a relationship with Him. Jesus connects us with the Father through Himself.

Jesus told us to have faith in God. When we pray we know that the Father hears us.

> Jesus replied, Have faith in God [constantly]. I assure you *and* most solemnly say to you, whoever says to this mountain, "Be lifted up and thrown into the sea!" and does not doubt in his heart [in God's unlimited power], but believes that what he says is going to take place, it will be done for him [in accordance with God's will]. For this reason I am telling you, whatever things you ask for in prayer [in accordance with God's will], believe [with confident

trust] that you have received them, and they will be *given* to you. (Mark 11:22-24 AMP)

Jesus told us to trust God constantly and confidently – to trust Him in everything and in all that we do. This is the will of God.

Jesus told us to believe in God and exercise our faith in Him. We do this by believing that He exists and knowing that our prayers get results. When a righteous man or woman prays, much is accomplished. Believers pray according to the promises of God and they receive from God. I search His Word to pray accurately for what He wants for me. I will surrender my desires and will to Him if I am not sure. "Lord, protect me from making stupid decisions and provide for me as You want. Please do as You see fit to do. Thank you Lord."

This is an exciting scripture portion in Mark 11. At times, we have to speak to things like mountains, rainstorms, sickness and especially the harassment of the devil. Other times. we talk to God just for the reason of speaking to and hearing from God.

In his writing, John Piper summed up prayer like this:

> "Then the line of prayer enters the heart of God, who is there listening, waiting for the prayers of his people. And in response to the prayers of the many Corinthians, God sends down a gift — or a "blessing," as the text says — to Paul. What blessing? Greater faith in God, greater dependence on him alone, and deliverance from his adversaries."

God hears and listens to our prayers. He does this because He cares. This text portion from John Piper talks about the blessings of having a greater reliance upon Him. We develop and become more dependent upon Him. As we depend upon Him more and more, we learn to receive His blessings in everything we do.

Realizing our dependence upon God comes as we renew our minds. (Romans 12:2) In this renewal, we leave the evil things of the world and enter into a life of the good things of God. We start to understand that without God in our lives through Jesus Christ, we are nothing. God Himself makes us a new creation in Christ and we renew our minds through reading and living what the Bible tells us. It is the wonderful Word of God. We spend time with God (fellowship) and we talk to Him (prayer). This relationship that we develop shows our absolute dependence upon Him.

The disciples finally began to understand about relying on God as they received the Holy Spirit and matured in God. This became apparent on the day of Pentecost when Peter preached and God saved many people. This same power occurred when Peter and John went to the Temple and were used in healing the crippled man.

Since believers today are also disciples of Christ, they become aware of God's reality and presence as they pray and learn from Him. The answer to our absolute need of Christ becomes clear as we begin understanding our experience with Christ. We seek and live for Him and we grow in Him. Today, let's make the choice to seek God and live for Him. Let's follow the leading of the Holy Spirit as we seek Him.

Now it's all clear.

Chapter Questions for Discussion or Study

1. Why did Jesus teach using parables?

2. FILL-IN: The parables are _____ when they are read. These stories help make the idea that is being taught _____ _____.

3. What happens when a believer studies the parables?

4. Why are believers now able to speak directly to the Father?

5. FILL-IN: Jesus said that we now _____ and _____ to the Father. I can talk to the Father _____, _____ and for any _____.

6. Jesus told us to have faith in God. What will happen if we exercise our faith in Him? (Mark 11:22-24)

7. Why does God hear and listen to our prayers?

8. When we renew our minds (Romans 12:2), how does our dependence on God increase?

9. FILL-IN: Since believers today are also disciples of _____, believers become aware of the _____ and presence of God as they _____ and learn from Him.

John 16 Chapter 8 You Will Be Scattered

People are scattered for many reasons. This often seems like a tragedy. God never gets rid of a believer (He does not forsake people). He does not "throw them on the trash heap."

> Jesus answered them, "Do you now believe? Indeed the hour is coming, yes, has now come, that you will be scattered, each to his own, and will leave Me alone. And yet I am not alone, because the Father is with Me. These things I have spoken to you, that in Me you may have peace. In the world you will have tribulation; but be of good cheer, I have overcome the world." (John 16:31-33 NKJV)

This passage speaks specifically about the night when Jesus would be arrested and the disciples would abandon Him. But scattering applies to God in the life of the believer.

The word *scattered* used in this passage means to *fly in every direction* or *disperse*. The scattering of people involves God sending and placing them where He needs and wants them to be. *Scattering* is seen when a farmer distributes (casts) seed in a field without regard to where each seed lands. (Mark 4:26) When a farmer *scatters* seed, he wants all of the seed dispersed throughout the plowed field.

Later, many of the disciples were scattered from Jerusalem to carry the Gospel of Jesus Christ to the people.

> Meanwhile, the believers who had been scattered during the persecution after Stephen's death traveled as far as Phoenicia, Cyprus, and Antioch of Syria. They preached the word of God, but only to Jews. However, some of the believers who went to Antioch from Cyprus and Cyrene began preaching to the Gentiles about the Lord Jesus. The power of the Lord was with them, and a large number of these Gentiles believed and turned to the Lord. (Acts 11:19-21 NLT)

The death of Stephen caused this scattering of the believers. He was stoned to death, which caused the persecutors to become bold. This boldness inspired deadly harassment.

God did not send this persecution against the disciples, but He used it to spread the good news of Jesus Christ. Following Jesus caused the scattering and the Gospel was spread outside Jerusalem.

> But you will receive power *and* ability when the Holy Spirit comes upon you; and you will be My witnesses [to tell people about Me] both in Jerusalem and in all Judea, and Samaria, and even to the ends of the earth. (Acts 1:8 AMP)

This persecution and scattering sent them in the power of the Holy Spirit to many places, including "the ends of the earth."

I live in central Virginia, north of Richmond. However, I was born near Detroit, Michigan and grew up there. After graduating from Michigan State University, I finally found a teaching job. But the position was in Spotsylvania County, Virginia - far away from my home and in a place I had never even heard of. I would have to move from my hometown and relocate. I was excited but felt scattered.

I did not feel that I was here permanently for a while, but I had plans to return "home" to

Michigan. Finally, I understood that I was <u>supposed</u> to be in Virginia – my scattering was a sending. God had a purpose for my life and I needed to obey and fulfill His desires. I became rooted in a GREAT Bible-believing church with caring pastors and started my journey of faith and growth in the Lord Jesus Christ. I learned that obeying God is better than pursuing my ideas, my self-created dreams and goals. Finding and doing God's will was a high calling, far above everything else.

I was saved, but I felt scattered. I was destined to know God and make Him known to the world. My friend Jesus had different goals for me than I had. I have found down through the years, that obedience to God is better than any sacrifice we make.

The scattering is also seen in the life of Paul. He persecuted the church and was traveling to Damascus to arrest Christians. Paul was determined, but God had something new that was far greater. The new outcome would change everything for Paul because it was infinitely more powerful.

God knocked Paul down while traveling on the road to Damascus (Acts 9) and changed his life. Jesus got ahold of Paul and he grew in the grace and knowledge of our Lord and Savior Jesus Christ. (2 Peter 3:18a NLT) Paul's existing life was immediately shattered when he became saved and a new creation in Christ. God called him to go to the Gentiles and reach them for Christ.

Paul traveled and preached extensively. He shared and won people to Christ and planted churches full of Gentile believers. In all of this, the message of Christ was sent throughout the known world. The Gospel spread to many people in many places because it truly was "good news"!

These different examples of the believers being scattered brought about the catalyst for change. The Christian Church was birthed among the disciples and followers of Jesus. It grew to several thousand and was mainly located in Jerusalem. As we saw, the Gospel was carried from Jerusalem "to all the world" and radically changed the lives of believers.

God turns all of our bad situations and challenges for our good. I have taken jobs because of pride and money – these are <u>not</u> good reasons for pursuing a new job or anything else. My rebellion and disobedience to God had a negative ending.

We have learned that obedience to the Father is what Jesus always practiced and lived. This is what I should have done - learn the Father's will and follow it accurately. God will guide us by His Spirit through the Word of God and bring His revelation to each of us.

> And we know that God causes everything to work together for the good of those who love God and are <u>called according to his purpose</u> for them. (Romans 8:28 NLT, emphasis added)

I loved God but was not obeying His will. God was merciful and rescued me and brought me back into His will. I didn't fully understand it at the time, but now, a few years later, I can see my disobedience and His working. God in His mercy rescued Paul and He will do it for you.

My bad decisions had a scattering effect on my life. It took God's intervention to fix things. God repaired me and restored my life back into obedience to Him.

In closing, I think of the song *To Be Used of God*. It's a beautiful song of a person who has their aspirations correctly aligned with God's purposes.

> *To be used of God, to sing, to speak, to pray;*
>
> *To be used of God to show someone the way.*
>
> *I long so much to feel the touch*
>
> *Of His consuming fire;*

To be used of God is my desire.

Allow God to use you today. Ask Him what to do and then follow Him.

Chapter Questions for Discussion or Study

1. Read Deuteronomy 31:8. Does God get rid of people? Why?

2. Do you think the farmer scattering seed is a good example of God scattering people? Why?

3. When Stephen was stoned to death, the disciples were scattered. Describe how this scattering helped carry the Gospel to people.

4. Paul had his life radically changed when Jesus confronted him on the road to Damascus. How was this a scattering? How did this scattering help bring the Gospel to all of the world?

Do you know Jesus?

I hope you enjoyed reading *Another Red Letter Day*. But more than that, I hope you heard from God and were inspired to seek a closer relationship with Jesus.

The BIG question is, "Do you know Jesus?" Many people would say yes, that He is the Son of God. This is the correct answer. But I am asking if you have more than knowledge of the fact of <u>who</u> Jesus is – do you know Him? Do you have a relationship with Him?

The scriptures tell us that if we admit and speak (confess) that "Jesus is <u>my</u> Lord and Savior and I believe the fact that God resurrected Him from being dead to being alive," I will be saved. This is the initial action that brings about the establishment of <u>our</u> relationship with Him. This is how we are saved.

Pray this prayer today.

> Jesus, I want to know you as my Lord and have a relationship with You. I realize that I am a sinner and need forgiveness from you. I accept you today as the boss of my life and accept you as

> my savior. Thank you Lord for saving me. Thank you for being my Lord. Amen.

If you prayed that with a sincere heart, you have been born again. You now have a relationship with God through your Lord and Savior, Jesus Christ.

I want to welcome you to becoming a Christian, to your new life in Jesus Christ. The scriptures teach us that we are NEW – the old is gone and the new has come!

> This means that anyone who belongs to Christ has become a new person. The old life is gone; a new life has begun! (2 Corinthians 5:17 NLT)

Get a Bible and read it. Find and attend a church that teaches and follows the Bible. Talk to God – this is prayer.

Be blessed and have faith and trust in God!